AN AUTUMN'S JOURNEY

Deep Growth in the Grief and Loss of Life's Seasons

CRAIG D. LOUNSBROUGH
M.DIV, LPC

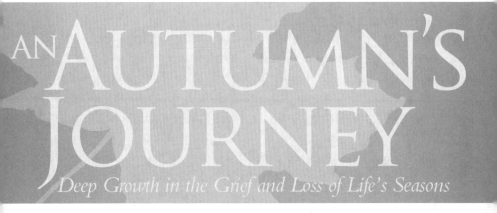

AN AUTUMN'S JOURNEY

Deep Growth in the Grief and Loss of Life's Seasons

CRAIG D. LOUNSBROUGH
M.DIV, LPC

AMBASSADOR INTERNATIONAL
GREENVILLE, SOUTH CAROLINA & BELFAST, NORTHERN IRELAND

www.ambassador-international.com

AN AUTUMN'S JOURNEY

Deep Growth in the Grief and Loss of Life's Seasons

© 2011 Craig D. Lounsbrough

Printed in the United States of America

ISBN: 978-1-935507-58-1

Cover Design & Page Layout by David Siglin of A&E Media

Edited by Kacie Dalton

AMBASSADOR INTERNATIONAL
Emerald House
427 Wade Hampton Blvd.
Greenville, SC 29609, USA
www.ambassador-international.com

AMBASSADOR BOOKS
The Mount
2 Woodstock Link
Belfast, BT6 8DD, Northern Ireland, UK
www.ambassador-international.com

The colophon is a trademark of Ambassador

Dedication

This book is the compilation of a two-year journey. It's hardly a summation, as grief and loss by their very nature continually shape us, always leaving some sort of sustained footprint. However, it does represent the journey as it was walked, felt, and engaged.

It would not have been a possible journey if it were not for the treasures Mom ingrained and rooted in the lives of her three boys through the immense sacrifices made in hers. Neither would this book have been possible were it not for her death, as that death forced me to draw from and lean upon those treasures. I therefore dedicate this book to Donna A. Lounsbrough, an exemplary mother in every way and manner. Thank you, Mom. I can't wait for that marvelously grand reunion.

The arduous and sometimes seemingly impossible journey of writing out my own grief and loss was motivated and sustained by my children. Their lives are an inspiration, a beacon that reminds me how good two young people can be and how much hope there is for the future. Therefore, I likewise dedicate this book to Cheyenne and Corey. Were it not for the two of you, this book would have never happened. You guys are the best!

Finally, a thanks to all of those at Ambassador International. I cherish your partnership and vision.

Table of Contents

Introduction

LOSS—IT TRIGGERS SOMETHING IRREPARABLY DEEP and central to our humanity. It reminds us that life is both a journey and a battle. We would prefer life to be a journey only, if not a consistently joyous one. Loss reminds us that life is more often a battle that at times can be ruthless, encompassing, and devastating. In the throes of loss we are inundated with the sense that life was not supposed to be this way, but it is nonetheless.

Loss has been my unwanted and uninvited companion on many occasions, as it has been for each of us. But this one occasion rendered all my other losses as something a bit less biting and slightly less black in comparison. Certain losses are weighted in this manner.

Although somewhat weak physically for several years, Mom experienced a situation that resulted in a rapid and confusing decline in her health. This decline was drawn out over the period of a month and was interspersed with assurances that she would recover, followed by tangled questions and near-misses. In the end, death took her. That was to be the conclusion of the matter.

In the convulsions of that month, as well as the death that was to follow, there was a provoking yet compelling need within me that strove to make sense of this, to build into and out of this experience something that made the experience worthwhile and gave it meaning. It seemed more than loss: that within this time and this loss there lay priceless clues to life and doors to a deeper understanding regarding this journey that we're all on.

In time there emerged a profound richness that did not take away the pain or erase the loss. Rather, it provided something of inestimable value that seemed to be complete only if it were shared with others.

Over the next two years the book that you hold in your hands came together. It took those two years to fully understand, assimilate, hone, and sharpen the thoughts, perspectives, and bits of insight that lie sown in these pages. Hopefully they will take root in your life and your loss in order that you might see something grand in something grievous.

The first thoughts put to paper regarding my loss were those written on an airplane from Denver, Colorado, to Toledo, Ohio, on October 19, 2007. With a window seat affording me a spectacular view of autumn at 34,000 feet, the words below were penned as a eulogy that was read at my mother's funeral one day later on October 20th. This was the beginning of my journey with loss. Hence, it seems an appropriate place to begin this book as well. May God bless you, bring you hope, gather you into His greater plan and grant you balm for healing in the pages of this book.

Saturday, October 20, 2007

Dear Mom,

At times like this, people tend to wax nostalgic, venerating those who have died. It is, I suppose, a courtesy to those who have passed, realizing that there is really no good sense in describing faults at the end. Rather, respect would dictate an honorable closure, granting the person dignity in death. Mom, I want you to know that the words that follow were carefully chosen, being written on behalf of your three sons with an intense commitment to celebrating the actual life that you lived, and doing so honestly as you would have wanted it. May these few minutes be pleasing to you, Mom, and may they represent yet another gift from you to the lives seated here today.

Mom, for the first time in the entirety of our lives, you are not here. The void is entirely new. It is an odd paradigm, knowing that you are running, racing, and resting in a place more glorious and perfect than our minds can hope to grasp. You are missed here. Yet if it were our choice, if your three boys had the power and authority to choose, even then we would not wish you here for you are truly home in a truly perfect and inexplicable way.

Mom, your voice here is now muted, heard only in our hearts, our memories, and throughout the grand halls of heaven. Even so, we hear it well. Your wisdom now arises from the many footprints you left across the landscape of our lives, examples that speak life and truth and love and ceaseless hope into both the barren places, as well as those places wonderful and lush that we walk through daily. Your touch is lost to us, those simple hugs from a simple woman who not only knew how to love, but how to express it in a way that made each moment warm and safe. It is one thing to be loved. It is quite another to know that you are loved. We knew and we know. We have lost so very much.

But, Mom, in the balance we have gained infinitely more. You have left a legacy in our lives, a legacy that embodies integrity, honesty, and tenacity. A legacy that boldly, even brashly, believes that God always provides, always cares, always knows, and is an ever present source from which every need will always be met. You helped us understand that life ebbs and flows, sometimes magically and sometimes cruelly. Life at times invites us to a grand dance; at other times it seems to slam us to the dance floor, leaving us cringing and bleeding. Life pours into us, and then draws out of us. The sun at times warms us, and then the hail pelts us. In whatever form it takes, you taught us that God always prevails, that there is always good, that it will always, always work out. And it always did.

You left us an understanding that life is more than some daily routine, or the achievement of tasks either great or small. Life is about living well, living with respect, living in a manner that adds rather than detracts. It is not about pretending things are well or being Pollyannaish. You taught us that life is about understanding that things will not always be fair nor will life necessarily be just, but in the hands of God it will always present us with opportunities to learn about ourselves, to grow, and to add something to those around us.

Mom, all of these lessons came packaged in simple things like iced tea on sweltering summer days and hot chocolate on frigid winter nights. It was bedtime prayers that started "now I lay me down to sleep . . . ." It was endless lunches packed for school, dimes tucked in lunchboxes for white milk during the week and chocolate milk on Fridays. It was planting flowers in spring's sweet soils and canning fruit when the season gradually but inevitably rolled over into fall. It was wrapping us thick in mounds of coats and scarves when winter drew nature to sleep, and vacuuming the pool when the glory of summer ran and skipped through our days. It was summed up in a tiny plaque that still hangs in the kitchen which reads, "Bless this house oh Lord we pray, make it safe by night and day." Such was your life.

It was being home when the street lights came on, carrying the laundry up the stairs, not hitting your brother, "Quit teasing the dog," "This didn't get broken by itself," "Did you call your grandmother?" "If your friends jumped off a cliff would you follow them?" "Would you please flush the toilet?" "Did you get your homework done?" "Please put your clothes down the dirty clothes chute," "Don't listen to your brother," "Who left the lights on?" "Please pick up your room," "Were you born in a barn?" "I didn't raise you kids to be like this," "Who tipped over the Christmas tree?" and "It didn't walk away by itself."

Underlying it all, being spoken with undeniable clarity, there were these messages . . . "I love you," "You can achieve anything you want with your life," "You kids are God's gift to me," "You're the best kids in the world," "I don't deserve you boys," "I'm praying for you," "How can I help you?" "How are you doing?" "Do you need anything?" and "I'm so proud of you boys." It was all of those things, and so much more.

Mom, you were about the stuff of building the lives of three boys and taking care of a husband who was at times a boy himself. It was really never about you. We tried to make it so many times, but you always declined. Rather, it was a selfless investment, pouring your life, your energies, and fiber of your being into three boys who really had no clue what you were doing until they themselves were adults. Even today, we are unable to fully fathom your sacrifices. I doubt that we will ever understand them fully.

We commit to you this day that we will strive to selflessly pour into the lives of others that which you so graciously poured into our lives. We know that any such efforts on our parts will pale indeed to the way in which you poured yourself into our lives. Know that we are committed to drawing from the innumerable footprints that you left, the lessons taught and lived, and the insights imparted. We will draw from the vast storehouse of memories packed tight with words, mental pictures, ceaseless emotions, and warm thoughts. And we will live that out, Mom, as we have for so many years. We will bring your life to our families, the people who populate our careers, and to those we meet in the briefest passing. You will live on, Mom, here as well as in the marbled halls of heaven. You will touch innumerable lives through your three boys who you loved, equipped, nurtured, guided, and guarded.

One final thing, Mom: we want you to know that we will live each day in anticipation of seeing you again. We commit that we will not let that anticipation somehow diminish the efforts and energies we invest in living life. We will not live in some sort of distracted state, focused solely on the idea of seeing you again and awaiting that moment in such a way that the present moment is squandered. Rather, we will invest our lives energetically while holding fast to the promise of scripture that there awaits for us a grand reunion, a wild celebration of relationships restored in a creation likewise restored. In the meantime, Mom, know that you are loved, that you are fondly remembered, that you live on in us, and that when stories of you are told, they will be told with the greatest love and admiration.

Thanks, Mom. We love you more than simple words could hope to convey. God bless. See you soon.

—Love,
Craig, Mark, and Brett

CHAPTER I

The Colors Turn Early:
Grief as Premature Loss

It is not for you to know the times or dates the Father has set by his own authority.
—Acts 1:7 (NIV)

IT'S EIGHT FEET AT BEST, if even that. When you're a kid, you run with the natural assumption that life will fall in your favor. It grants exceptions and kind of looks out for you. You think of life as some sort of doting grandparent and adventurous friend all in one, inviting you out to wild, frolicking play while hovering close enough to catch you if you fall. It's the best of both worlds, of all worlds really. It makes life terribly wild and inordinately safe all at the same time. So, it's only eight feet. The next limb up was probably another four feet at least. That was a stretch. But eight feet; that was just about perfect.

We had spent days raking those leaves, several days. Pungent remnants of a summer nudged off fall's calendar. We had raked them when they were still electric: royal golds, velvety reds, and sizzling oranges. Covered in pigments liberally scattered from an artist's pallet, the ground had been magically transformed to a patchwork potpourri of splendor on a canvas of faded summer grasses. We hated to rake it up really, to desecrate the canvas. But the passion for fun prevailed and so they were raked into massive piles, clearing summer's faded canvas to wait for a distant spring.

It was only eight feet. But with both the wild child and protective grandparent of life begging us to jump, we could do no other. Eight feet is only eight feet. But when you're a child entirely wrapped warm in the embrace of the wild and protection of life, you leap, you plummet in a manner that feels much more like flying through a trackless sky fully abandoned to the gracious mercy of life . . . and then you land.

It seemed that you fell forever, but it was all terribly immediate at the same time. Both the vast endlessness and terrific brevity of it wove a puzzling dichotomy, giving the eight-foot plummet two sides and providing me two entirely unique experiences at the very same time. It seemed part of life's mystical ability to be inexplicably different and wildly divergent about a single experience, God being relentlessly fresh every time He touches us.

In the landing, at that very moment, the exhilaration of the entire adventure distills itself into some sort of crazy tonic that instantly saturates your brain, electrifying every neuron with emotion. And there, gazing up eight feet to the branch above and another fifty feet to the massive canopy that bequeathed these leaves, life surges with tsunami force within you. You can't move but all you want to do is move. It's incredible, and it is good.

Off in the distance, the last of autumn's leaves pirouette from trees now heavy with fall's slumber. The breeze has turned a bit brisk, slightly seasoned by the chilled hand of an approaching winter. Birds gathered en masse as throbbing clouds of aviary sojourners bouncing south under heavy skies.

It was only eight feet, but the descent and the landing dramatically sharpened the senses to allow every ounce of fall's vitality to surge in all at once. Life becomes so electrifying that you have to shut it off or you feel that you'll explode from the inside out. And so, it's back up the tree for another eight feet of wonder.

And Then Adulthood

Decades evaporate, and over four of them rushed by in a blur of time and events. Columns of stately maples, elms, and oaks stood at attention, woodland sentries stoutly ringing a small, broad pond. Its glassy expanse thinned in the middle, drawing its banks close enough to permit a small bridge to cast a slight arch across its tepid waters. A slight chill permeated the air. Tentative but timely, the thin crispness was just strong enough to hint at the turn of the season on that mid-October day. Yet it was sufficiently subtle to cull a rich aromatic delight from the first of freshly fallen leaves. Fall was back . . . early.

Fall had come quietly that year, unobtrusively, as if heeding something reverent and austere. The leaves held a bit that October. Slightly pausing, they turned from summer's tired green to the exuberant blaze of fall. They seemed to hold their canopies close, refusing to fully surrender to a season turning on the axis of the year. Life, it seems, is so very profuse that even the pending death ever engulfing me was muted and restrained in the swell. It's breathtaking and life-taking all at once. Mom was dying. Fall had turned another side to me that I had never before known or wished to know. The plunge was infinitely more than the eight feet of childhood. This time the descent was as endless as the emotional freefall of her dying felt bottomless. The wonder of that season remained, but it has become tightly woven and inseparable with the loss in the turning.

The doting grandparent and adventurous friend seem to have backed away, if not disappeared altogether. "To grow up is to accept vulnerability... To be alive is to be vulnerable" (Madeleine L'Engle). Yet vulnerability is exacting and devastating, especially when the colors turn early.

Mallards slid from low-slung fall skies, cutting smooth lines in the glassy surface of the pond and sending glistening ripples in the same V-formations that these waterfowl had drawn across a graying firmament. With the momentum of migration propelling them, they skimmed under the wooden bridge's span and briefly settled on fall's waters, preening translucent feathers before fall called them back to her skies.

The ornate bridge's sturdy wooden beams and gently curved rails invited the grieving to pause over reflective waters. Death invites lingering and pondering. It provokes it as death raises innumerable and terribly tangled questions about life. Death is a reality that calls the rest of life and all of our assorted strivings into sharp relief, begging dark and foreboding questions. It forces the questions that we are able to deftly deny . . . until death comes. And death had come unexpectedly that fall, ramming the fist of adulthood squarely against the sweet memories of wild laughter and eight-foot plunges. The disparity was stunning and wholly paralyzing.

Several figures lingered on the bridge's broad oak and maple spine. They too wrestled with death, giving us a shared experience that mystically forged comrades from complete strangers. A hospice wrapped in fading gardens invited such pondering and the melding that results from a mutual experience.

Strolling the bridge's oak span, they paused over glassy waters in a momentous struggle to understand how something as final as death figures into the exuberance of life. Behind them leaves pirouetted and avian voyagers charted paths southward as always, but there was a sharp relief of what the child side of me wished to grasp in the momentum of fall and what the adult side of me was mercilessly forced to deal with.

I stood a short distance away at the edge of a sandy bank generously hemmed with dried reeds and brittle cattails that tiptoed through glistening shallows. Even from there, I felt the thoughts of those on the bridge as sharp and leaden as if they were my own. How does it all work, this life and death thing? How does it hold itself against all the wonder of life to which it seems so contradictory? The suddenness and incongruity of it all pressed upon me with a blackened vigor; I found myself standing in a slumped stupor weighed by forces and crushed by realities that descended without notice or warning. How does it all work, the beauty and tragedy of life? A hospice created a place where such questions were gently entertained in lives where those questions were now being forced.

Tinges of fall color in the surrounding forest reflected in the mirrored surface, dancing on the slight wakes of arriving geese and shimmering when a passive breeze gently rippled the calm waters. Hedges of blueberries and tangles of wild grape filled in the forest floor, hemming in this place of wonder and solace. Inside the hospice, a few feet from that pond and the surrounding woods, my mother was dying . . . quickly, unexpectedly, and without remedy. Nature itself was turning in what was always her favorite season of the year. That fall, she would depart with it. Even though I was desperate to do so, I could no more hold on to her than stop the roll of the season turning in front of me.

Grand and Grievous All at Once

How can life be so terribly grand and so utterly grievous at the same time? I sat but a handful of feet away from a dying mother and attempted to reconcile this most glorious season with a suffocating loss that pressed my heart with such weight that it labored to pound out each precarious beat. Yet I was at the same time drawn back to an eight-foot jump in the arms of a wild grandparent who always bade me gracious favors and loving protection. I saw nature in spectacular display all around me with forested vistas rolling off to vividly painted horizons. Yet, in front of me there walked those whose faces were veiled ashen in the pending death of a loved one.

How do you reconcile it all? I wanted to believe that life was either good or bad. In resting in one or the other I freed myself of the gargantuan task of having to believe in both. In doing that, I removed the hideous disappointment that befell me when the bad prevailed, and I kept myself safe from unsustainable joy and hope when the good abounded. Either way, I know that one or the other will seize the landscape of my life and just as quickly leave it to the other. I would simply prefer to rest in one rather than have to alternate between both. I was falling much farther than a mere eight feet, and the exhilaration of it all had turned terribly black.

My mother was dying. The juxtaposition between an eight-foot fall and a mother's death was entirely unfathomable. I sat at the pond's edge, groping to seize and hold close the wonder of life on one side in order to believe that life makes sense and that good is sustained even in great and terrible pain . . . or more so, in great evil. On the other side, with great trepidation I tried to reach out and touch the pain ringing both cold and hollow, knowing that I could not deny it nor could I ignore it.

An eight-foot drop and a dying mother seemed as from horizon to horizon in distance from one another, yet I knew that I had to embrace them both. Sitting by that pond, I could not span the gapingly impossible expanse.

It was here, in these places, that we realize the vast dichotomy of life. At one end of the created framework there are set intoxicating joys that exhilarate and enthuse us to the end of our emotions and beyond. At the other end there looms the specter of devastating pain and chillingly dark moments. Life embodies both of these dramatic extremes. And at times we are helplessly tossed between both of them.

Managing the vastness of life is about managing our response to it. When the colors turn early and the riotous leaps of eight feet turn bottomless, we can choose our disposition and thereby navigate these extremes. Martha Washington wrote, "I am still determined to be cheerful and happy, in whatever situation I may be; for I have also learned from experience that the greater part of our happiness or misery depends upon our *dispositions, and not upon our circumstances* [italics mine]."

More than navigating these extremes simply to survive, we can put ourselves in a position to effectively savor this vast dichotomy of life. We live in a world of immense and incomprehensible variety. Incredibly, we are shaped and created with the capacity to fully embrace, experience, and incorporate the full depth and breadth of that marvelous diversity. In the embracing, we can experience the vastness of life as both dark and light, subsequently growing in ways unimaginable while managing the venture by choosing our disposition. I prefer eight-foot leaps, but I likewise see the opportunity in bottomless falls.

Turns That Leave the Precious Behind

As I peered over the pond and out to the deep woods beyond, the seasons were changing. Life was rolling on, leaving behind something immensely precious. Nearly, it seems, discarding something it should not. At times life seems insensitive, casting aside that which yet has some remnant of life remaining. Something seems incomplete, a resource not yet exhausted, something seized and stolen before its time.

Sometimes life seems unfinished, the edges not yet sanded smooth, the final touch not yet rendered on a canvas bathed in colors of near perfection, a finish line not yet crossed swelling with applause and exhilaration. It simply should not be over. So it seems. There should be more eight-foot leaps to make, but eventually there will be the final jump. And it had come.

Sometimes completion is not what we think it to be. We hold some idea of what something will look like when it's complete or has fulfilled its purpose. We apply a standard that in most cases is terribly inferior to the perfect destiny for which this person or this time or this thing had been created. We see the loss of the moment and are blinded to the larger purpose. Life tips on finely orchestrated events that vastly supersede our comprehension. Jesus uttered, "It is finished" (John 19:30 NIV), to an event that his followers could not believe should have finished in that manner. In their minds something was not completed, yet it was completed perfectly.

Grieving acknowledges completion. Whether we can see it or not, it's resting in the belief that there is a completion that gives sense, meaning, and a rationale to our loss. Completion means that anything more is unnecessary. That loss is not about a future now stolen. It takes unfairness away and replaces it with an appropriate closure.

Twice Stolen

In the taking, it's all relegated to the whimsy of memory. Memory is what's left after something's over. It seems wholly incapable of fully holding on to the thing that it's attempting to recall. It's but a lean shadow, a thinning recollection of something marvelous and grand. Memory can only hold a piece of that which we lose. In the holding, it often takes artistic license and amends the memory so that it's either less painful or visually richer. In either case, it's easier to hold. So when we lose something wonderful, in great part we lose a great part of it forever.

Goldfinches and orioles skirted the woods' edge and lighted on bustling feeders hanging sturdy at the bridge's edge. Having been left far behind the hem of a summer long thrown off the edge of the hemisphere, they reminded me of a season past . . . remnants of what was. Summer itself walked with us through lush green days, caressing us with warm kisses of new life. It granted us sultry nights bespeckled with galaxy upon galaxy of stars packed into its rotund, velvety canopy. It begged us to smell dandelions, to run sandy beaches, to roll in mounds of wildflowers, to ascend the muscular limbs of maple and aspen, to climb lofty peaks, and to wonder in a way that makes reveling sublime.

It was all fading now, relegated to the back alleys of my mind, conjured up in anemic images void of the flurry and flourish, of scent and the sacred. But its time was over even though we presumed there to be more life to be had. Summer had more to give it seems. But sometimes the colors change early.

Inside this hospice, a few steps from fall itself, my mother was passing just like summer was passing. From the inside of her room, her window framed the glorious scene of transition unfolding in front of me. But from the outside looking in, this same window only served to frame her in death. She had yet to draw her final breath, although it was terribly close. Already the images of her were fading. Already she was passing into the far corridors of my mind, cloaked in ever deepening shadow before I felt she should. Already the tone of her voice, soft around the edges, was becoming muffled. Already her gestures, her mannerisms and smile, her tone and touch, the dancing, crystalline blue eyes so full of life were slipping as turning wisps of smoke through my fingers. I couldn't remember the eight-foot fall anymore although I was desperate to do so.

"Now we see only a reflection as in a mirror" (I Corinthians 13:12 NIV), says Paul as he squints, cants his head a bit, and gazes into the next life. I saw but a poor reflection gazing at this life as it unfolded inside a window where the colors were turning early. Already I was grieving not being able to hold her or the memories so poignant and sweet. The colors were indeed turning earlier than I presumed they should. But colors were turning anyway.

Turns of Life Turning Forward

"I go to prepare a place for you" (John 14:2 ASV), says Jesus. "No man, having put his hand to the plow, and looking back, is fit for the kingdom of God" (Luke 9:62 ASV). "I came out from the Father . . . and go unto the Father" (John 16:28 ASV).

Jesus' actions in the present were all about the future . . . that time which stands a nanosecond in front of us and beyond the larger season that we call today. Out there is something called eternity, that thing which seasons cannot define or contain. Eternity is the future infinitely multiplied against itself. It's the ultimate destination that always held Jesus' gaze, yet it didn't hold mine as much as I wish it did.

Was this season over? Was eternity rushing upon my mother? Or was that all simply a marginalized perspective drawn tight by blinders of fear or absence of vision or thinness of faith?

In actuality, it's a step into something that will never be over. Eternity is the end of the end. There are no more endings there. The end of this life is the beginning of an endless eternity of ceaseless beginnings. And so, is the end really an end, or the beginning of that which will never end? Is eternity the extermination of even the notion of an end? Then we are obligated, if not forced, to ask, What is more in death: loss or gain? Are we losing something, or is what we're gaining so vast and terribly grand that it essentially wipes out any loss whatsoever? Does it eclipse eight-foot jumps?

Does it matter . . . really? Was it suggestive of a past now being lost before its time, or was it a past being set aside upon which an endless future was to be built? Was it about the limits that the past imposes upon us because its story is unchangeable history written in incomplete relief, or was it about the limitlessness of a future as a story yet to be crafted, formed, and told that will not be held hostage to whatever the past was or was not? Was life about a checklist of accomplishments completed and thoroughly marked off with some prescribed tedium? Or was it about joining a much more vast adventure that is not defined by our expectations, but by the hand of a God who perfectly brings every life to closure at the perfect time in order to seize that exact adventure and set us out on horizonless hills? Will it make eight-foot jumps in the throes of childhood appear terribly minor by comparison? I think so.

How It All Fits

My mother was dying. For the first time in my life I found myself caught between a past on the verge of a seeming premature passing and a future that I was not ready for. It was fall. October was slipping away and my mother with it. In it I felt both my dread of loss and my lack of faith in the future. If my mom didn't somehow figure into my future, any vision that I would cast instantly disintegrated into a bitter talcum that blew an acidic residue all around me. I couldn't let go because the past was fading fast, the future was inconceivable, and eternity was simply too incomprehensible.

Panic stricken, facing uncertainties behind and before, I held on to that which I couldn't hold on to without seeing both the promises for her and me. I sensed something infinitely grander, but at that raw place of unexpected loss I couldn't grasp it. I could see it all around me in the flush of a season celebrating death so that it could celebrate life. But the bridge that this created for me, much like the stout maple and oak arch that spanned the waters before me, was simply too difficult to cross. I edged up to its footing and I knew the passage that it called me to. I needed to cross. I wanted to cross. But I could go no further.

The Colors Are Turning

The leaves rustled in the wind, its fingers culling nature forward in both death and dance. It was an odd combination indeed . . . celebration and cessation all at once. A nonnegotiable bargain struck for us by the sin of the first man, a counter offer on a cross without which life would stall, stagnate, and eventually cease to be life. Seasons must turn. Season is built upon season in an escalating dance. Oddly, the cross itself was accomplished so that we can pass from the season of this life to the season of the next. On the cross, Jesus built the ultimate bridge. He jumped, but infinitely farther than eight feet.

Geese and an assortment of waterfowl moved in slight circles on glassy waters. Massive assemblages of birds skimmed the treetops as feathered aviaries on a mystical journey to southern skies. The grand arch of the sky lent itself gray and cold. Nature was beginning to tuck itself in. The colors were changing early and I was not ready.

I turned to leave. As I did, my gaze was drawn to a small metal plaque by the bridge. I stumbled upon the words that were etched there: "'For I know the plans I have for you,' declares the Lord, 'plans to prosper you and not to harm you, plans to give you *hope and a future*'" (Jeremiah 29:11 NIV, italics mine). I was and I am grateful for the promise, but I stood at both bridge and woods' edge, running fingers over the raised wording on this simple plaque but unable to claim its message. The colors were turning early and I was being prepared to let them turn. I was being prepared to let life go out of my reach, to let it all run ahead of me without me. Around me life was advancing in dark directions that were not of my creating. Yet I had to let it advance and in the advancing find some hope or rationale that would permit me to join it, to know that out there in terribly unpleasant places lay a hope and a future. I had to let go and I had to leap.

Chapter 2

Drawing Out of Reach:
Grief as Letting Our Losses Go

When you lose someone you love, you die too, and you wait around for your body to catch up.
—John Scalzi

DID YOU EVER RUN WITH leaves—a wild race born of wind and liberated foliage? It's a race, but more than that it's really an invitation to partnership and farewell. Racing with the leaves was not about finishing first; rather it was about a romp enjoyed in the midst of a transition being celebrated. It was playing with a friend before that friend was called away home.

It happened in fall's own autumn when the leaves turned dry. They had long lost their color, becoming curled and brittle, gnarled sometimes like hands beset with arthritis. Winter's impending snows skirted the horizon and teased the forecast. It was something like the last hurrah before fall slipped away. As a kid, it was an invitation to play one more time, to playfully challenge the remnant of leaves that had yet to sleep.

It most often began in the street as a brisk winter wind dove and spun from graying skies, slipping just centimeters over the asphalt. The myriad leaves strewn about seemed to grab hold for one final thrill, hitching a ride for one more bit of hilarity and fun. They raced, spun, and tumbled down the road, at points catching themselves in winter's eddies and spinning in perfect circles as if caught in a delirious waltz. Pooled in some sort of scripted conglomeration, they would suddenly burst forward en masse to continue their pell-mell race down the road.

For a kid, it was all too inviting. It was play and farewell all in one. You had to race, to run in some sort of camaraderie, or you felt that you were somehow betraying fall and being brutish about its departure.

And so we raced. It was playful enough until winter blew a briskly firm wind that sent jovial leaves bounding past us at a pace we could not match. Left behind in a deluge of wildness, we would pull up and stop, breathlessly watching the leaves hurl themselves down the street and into the bosom of winter. It was more than just leaves. Rather it was bidding a season farewell, watching it roil and dance down the street, turning back and waving goodbye as it went. Fall was drawing out of reach, leaving us behind to wait for the next season.

Breathless and aching, I felt it was a bittersweet moment—those times when you don't want to lose what you have while you're simultaneously looking forward to what's coming. It was about wanting to hold all things at all times, not in the sense of seasons, for seasons don't hold; rather they give and then take. We want all the accumulated good of life to be constantly present, rather than a good thing having to leave in order to make room for another good.

Kids don't understand goodbyes. I saw it all as kind of circular, that whatever I was losing would come back. Fall would come again. We'd race again. The hello and goodbye of this season would happen again and again. I did not embrace loss as permanent so it was easier to let go knowing it was eventually coming back. Kids don't understand that sometimes things leave forever, that finality has a nonnegotiable terminus where an end is indisputably an end often without apology or explanation. But I didn't know that. Fall was drawing out of reach only to return on the backside of next year's calendar. And so we waved goodbye to fall and ran wildly into winter.

Drawing Out of Reach in Adulthood

It wound in stilled wonderment past the sturdy walls of the hospice and around the pond, mystically inviting grieving passersby to a soulful stroll. Brushing the edge of a dense forest caught in the early stages of releasing fall's blaze, the brick path offered those on its gentle concourse the opportunity to brush the edge of their own existence as well. Death does that, and a hospice is a place for death.

The path was an artistic fusion of decorative bricks laid out in relentless mosaics. It was ever changing and always beautiful. Gracefully worn at the edges and framed in slight strings of emerald moss, the path was a brick menagerie aged and gentle. It wound around the entire pond, encircling the waters with a gentle but slightly distant embrace.

It had known the footsteps of many whose strides were made heavy with pending loss. Tears had mottled its surface. Sobs had run in rivulets deep into its crevices. The lamenting of lives lost and opportunities squandered had drawn the brickwork tight. Grief and celebration held simultaneously had prompted wonderment, the path often attempting to understand the contradiction. It had aged indeed but with the sturdy mantle of wisdom and the tender softness of a rare empathy. It didn't dominate but invited the passerby with muted whispers to a curious walk along the edge of life and death.

That Thin Line

The first of fall's leaves had begun to litter the path by the time my brother and I walked it. They wanted to race, but their invitation was more than we could heed. The invitation to frolic and farewell was the same, but I had no heart for it. Fall would be back. My mother would not. Fall drew out of reach every year only to return. As a kid, I didn't understand that sometimes things leave forever, that finality has a nonnegotiable terminus where an end is indisputably an end often without apology or explanation. Mom's departure would be permanent, without apology or adequate explanation.

The path seemed to weep as only true sympathy can beget weeping, brushing aside fallen leaves as so many tears, itself declining one more romp. Something about this path seemed thick and generous with empathy, somehow knowing our pain because of the pain of so many others whose steps and heartache still lingered in the crevices and cracks of its brickwork. It beckoned, inviting us to a contemplative stroll that took the mind beyond the simple hedgerows of the heart and deep into the wilderness of the soul.

Death invites us out there, beyond the comfort of life's edge. It seems that the thin line where life and death meet is a tempestuous and fearful place. One does not cross over only to return on the backside of some calendar. Goodbyes are not followed by hellos, at least none that happen on this side of that line. There was a foreboding permanence that this line was not circular; rather it was linear, moving on to something else someplace else.

A Glimpse of Both Worlds

This precarious line calls into question so many things we prefer not to call into question. Latent feelings lying deep within some sort of emotional substrata are awakened and rise despite our desire to keep them submerged. Edging up against our own humanity is always a frightening thing. Living in the denial or ignorance that finality is final allows us to live with a sense of the eternal in a world terribly temporal.

There is that inherited bit of eternity that lies deep within us that rails against the confines of the temporal, awakening a deep sense that we were originally designed for life without limits. When limits are laid out as lines across the landscape of our lives, much like that path, we find ourselves facing something that was not meant to be, but something that is anyway.

Yet, this line is filled with a sublime richness, handing out pearls of wisdom and priceless insights that give away, in some nearly magical way, some of life's most closely guarded secrets. It is here that the dichotomy of life and death, of the finite and the infinite, of the eternal and temporal edge up to each other and eventually intersect in one place. The two sides of life merge in a rare and uncanny way, giving us vast glimpses of the whole of existence.

Somehow winding down its broad path afforded the grieving the privilege of encountering a path not often traveled in both heart and spirit. Here the deep wood drew up shoulder to shoulder with the brick path, much as death and life draw shoulder to shoulder in such moments.

It was not a clash, but one aspect of life being fully present with the other likewise fully present, life standing side by side with death in a partnership of sorts. It was indeed the consummation of the entirety of existence, an extremely rare convergence where each inhabited a single place at a single moment. It was really not about anything waving goodbye only to say hello in the turn of some season. It was about the complete appropriateness of this finality as being the crowning touch to life. It was the need for a final exit that set the stage for a final entrance in a place where hello was in reality "welcome home," and "goodbye" would be eternally unknown and therefore entirely absent. Something surged within me as two aspects of the same thing came together on a simple brick path that wound tight against fall's wood.

Our Fear of the Line

I lived on the life side of that line, as far away from the line itself as possible so as to be as far from death as possible. My mother was drawing ever closer to that line, moving to cross from this side to the other. Her illness had thrust me to the edge of that demarcation, as a means of either keeping Mom from crossing over or attempting to see that the place she was heading toward was both prepared and fitting. I don't know. An illness had pushed her near the line when I was in kindergarten at a tender five years of age. Thankfully, she did not cross then, although she had brushed frighteningly close.

Now some four decades later, the crossing was imminent. There would be no return, no coming back on the backside of the calendar. Leaves blew down the tight brick path into a pending winter. I felt no urge to bid them farewell, nor did I feel brutish and insensitive by not doing so. The farewell that I was facing supplanted any desire for any farewell ever. Yet I attempted to grasp the appropriateness of a final farewell in exchange for a forever hello.

Other loved ones had crossed over this path . . . aunt and uncles and grandparents, descending into some sort of abyss that permitted no spectators, leaving me distanced by the fear of that place. From this side, I couldn't see what was there. Like the forest running deep and dense, death quickly drew those I loved out of sight behind veils of shadow into some place that I couldn't see. If there was life out there, I couldn't make it out. And if there was, could it ever possibly be as colorful as life on this side of that line? What was Mom crossing over to? Seizing the hem of a winter wind, the leaves bounded into the deep wood and cavorted out of sight.

The Known Unknown

"For I go to prepare a place for you" (John 14:2 ASV). Somewhere out there a place was prepared for Mom. Across that line that she was approaching lay a provision unknown to me. It was said to be spectacular, the stuff of mansions. But I wanted to see it to affirm it as being so in order to lend me some comfort. She was drawing out of reach. When you draw out of the reach of one place, you draw into the reach of another. However, I couldn't see that other place.

I held to the belief that whatever that place was like, it was magnificent. Magnificence begets mystery, somehow becoming so grand that it's too grand to be randomly disclosed. It is the stuff of privilege, holding secret its bounty until those destined for it see it for the first time. Grandeur disclosed in a sudden massive display is thrilling. I hoped that heaven was such a place. Despite the fact that I couldn't see it past the deep wood and shadows of life, I prayed that it was out there waiting for Mom in indescribable splendor, a welcome growing in wild anticipation of her arrival from which any departure would be eternally unnecessary.

Despite the wonder of all of that, my first and most fierce intent was to stop this crossing over, oddly railing against a journey I could not stop. Sometimes life appears to carry out its plan without seeming to cast an eye toward those affected by that plan. I felt alone and invisible, lost on a gentle brick path teased by parting leaves that wound around a quiet hospice.

Drawing Away and Fading

A number of the bricks embedded along the way contained inscriptions of names and dates etched deeply into their reddish clay surfaces. Some had filled with dirt and scattered speckles of moss, the footprints of time revealed in their growth. Others were entirely fresh and sharp, being new to this gentle path. Each name represented a history likely embellished with both wonder and tragedy, a story now completed and slipping with ever increasing vagueness into a misty past. They were inscriptions . . . a handful of letters shouting out names in brick and mortar relief, leaving the world one remaining voice that would forever speak the names of those who had died in this place.

The names cascaded through my mind as torrents of people whose faces I attempted to visualize and whose lives I found myself fabricating. They were entirely unknown to me. Yet, it seemed all too appropriate to resurrect them in my mind at least, to not allow death to draw them out of reach entirely. It seemed some primitive effort to minimize the power of this line by pulling a foggy fragment of these people back across to this side.

The brick path was a curious path, made for the living by those now dead, made so that the drawing away might not result in being entirely drawn from existence itself. It was an inevitable path, one that we all walk, skirting the immortal at one time or another. Some are in front of us along this path, others are behind, and yet others refuse to walk it even though not walking it is not an option. Life on one side and death on the other.

The record of those passing across that line were etched as whispers on fired clay beneath our feet so that names and lives would not be forgotten as they drew out into the deep wood. All of these names had drawn out of reach, leaving the single footprint sketched out in a handful of letters. These bricks held their ground while fall's leaves bounded over them and raced off to winter. Mom would cross this line. Her name and her life were already being etched across my heart.

The soles of our shoes scuffed the path's surface that day. We paid little attention to the support that it laid under us and the guidance it provided us. We were adrift in a mother drawing out of reach in this place of death. It is likely that the path served the most anonymous role conceivable, being a path upon which the grief of those walking it made the path entirely obscure. Mom was becoming obscure as was the entire scope of life itself. Yet this path gave us a footing that we didn't even recognize, much as God gives us a sure footing when what is precious and sacred is being drawn out of reach.

The Onset of Grief as the Inability to Stop Loss

Grief often begins before the loss impales us. Grief finds its origins in the anticipation of loss, and it deepens as we become increasingly convinced of the ruthless inevitability of the loss. At his most dire moment, Jesus uttered the plea, "If it be possible, let this cup pass away from me . . . ." (Matthew 26:39 ASV). His grief was related to what had not yet transpired. It was ground not in the loss itself, but in anticipating the loss.

It may be that anticipation of loss is something of guesswork and speculation, being our attempts to manage or deal with a pending loss. Sometimes it seems that we attempt to visualize loss as some sort of proactive strategy so that the fury or fire or ferocity of loss itself is contained before it befalls us. Such endeavors call for great speculation, thought, and a host of presumptions that frequently render the process itself in excess of the actual loss.

Likewise, it seems that grief arises from our inability to stop the loss. Our grief also appears grounded in the realization of our weakness as held against the enormity of what looms before us and our inability to coerce life into avoiding those things. It's that we can't stop loss. We're powerless before this thing called life. It will forcefully move through our days, our hours, and our most guarded core with no consideration for what costs its movement may incur. Often life pulls across this line and out of our reach the very things which we so desperately wish to hold on to. And Mom was drawing out of our reach.

Obedience and Understanding

Are we willing to be obedient to that which we may not understand? "As the heavens are higher than the earth, so are my ways higher than your ways and my thoughts than your thoughts" (Isaiah 55:9 NIV), declares God.

It's not about understanding the movements of God and creation. It's about finding some meaningful abandonment and embracing an entirely confident surrender to that which we can't grasp and therefore don't understand. We intentionally set ourselves squarely outside ourselves, allowing us to live in places we have no hope of comprehending, choosing to believe that there is no other place so grand to be. We realize that the vast majority of this thing we call life and all that makes life grand and massive and terribly exciting is out there, in a place that only God understands. And there, we are left without any understanding except that we are perfectly placed and at home more completely than in anything else this side of eternity.

It's impossible to find this place, much less reside there, unless we trust that in God's hands all is purposeful with a value far, even infinitely beyond whatever loss might be sustained. Is it a matter of fighting the pull of life or attempting to redirect the great torrents that come against us, to halt the army of departing leaves that race down the road and into winter? Or is it assuming control by the relinquishment of control? Is it seizing with a brash intentionality the belief that in the pulls, torrents, and torments God has a grand purpose if we only dare to look, ask, or step aside so that we can run to this place of faith, safety, and utter abandonment?

Paul wrote that "faith is confidence in what we hope for and assurance about what we do not see" (Hebrews 11:1 NIV). Faith is not about dissection or deductive thinking or rationalization or endeavors designed to rein the infinite into an intellectual corral where it can run itself in predictable circles. Faith is about deciding not to know. It's not about ignorance or the lack of commitment to gain and garner knowledge. Rather, it's about acknowledging that all knowledge will quickly collide with a grand wall which human intellect cannot scale, dismantle, or burrow under. It's acknowledging its presence and embracing, even seeking, its arrival. It's about knowing that the vast majority of life is surrender to what we can't know and a God Who we can. If we can do this, then when death comes and it moves into the shadows of the deep woods beyond our vision, we can accept it, embrace it, and in time even cheer it on.

But here lies the great defeating rub. The lynchpin upon which our thinking is prone to either lavish graciousness or unbridled hate is understanding, or lack thereof. We demand to know. Tell me about this crossing over. In light of its unfathomable permanence, explain its rationale and process to me! Show me how it fits and how it's the better option.

"It is not for you to know times or seasons, which the Father hath set within His own authority" (Acts 1:7 ASV). We hate that, particularly in crisis. It's not enough. It explains nothing. It asks me to believe without hard data or fast facts that would give me a reason and platform to believe. Our lack of faith demands the infusion of information. Information shapes an explanation. And we hope that the explanation is sufficient.

It's God's odd, seemingly incongruent dichotomy that we grow the best when we know the least. Lack of understanding provokes

faith and forces it. If we don't understand, we either seethe with re-
bellion or take a radical posture of resting in a grander plan whose
scope and breadth we simply cannot see or adequately apprehend.
Mom was drawing out of reach, and I was forced to the precipice of
this decision to demand to know or let it go. I found it easy in theory
but enormously taxing in reality. I wrestled with it imperfectly.

Beating Grief Equals Surrender

Is beating grief the wrestling with surrender and surrendering to surrender? Would grief not only be reduced, but possibly
abolished? Surrender is largely synonymous with abandonment
in the sense of abandoning our right to fear and embracing our
greater right to peace. "And the peace of God, which passeth all
understanding" (Philippians 4:7 ASV) is ours if we rest in surrender rather than the terrible angst of information that is always
insufficient in loss.

Surrender is a choice. As a choice, it is a privilege. We have the
privilege of surrendering to God. Surrender in a relationship with
God is not about defeat as we presume it to be. It is a supremely
tactical move vested in wisdom and faith.

In dealing with grief, it is handing over our lives and our pain
with the full acknowledgement that surrender to God means the
defeat of grief. "Not my will, but thine, be done" (Luke 22:42
ASV). It's not acknowledging our inadequacy; rather it is acknowledging God's adequacy. We move away from the need to
know and move toward the need to believe. Knowing is never
sufficient—genuinely believing always is.

Surrender is letting go to something infinitely bigger than I,
who sees a plan much bigger than the one I see. It's resting in
the conviction that the path unfolding before me is rich even
though its escarpment and ascent seem only the stuff of pain and

its glories largely obtuse. It frees me to set a course along that line between this life and the next, drawing into the lungs of my soul both halves of life as living and dying.

More profoundly, it's embracing the fact that Jesus crossed over this line into death and then of His own accord and power came back across this same line into life again. "He . . . is risen" (Luke 24:6 ASV): three simple words that are said of no one else in all of human history. Sometimes the grandest of all events are best described in the poverty of a few simple words. In a handful of syllables it was declared that Jesus crossed back over. He did both sides of it, and He controls both sides of it. He returned on the backside of the calendar. If indeed He controls both sides of this seemingly precarious line, then the line is really of no accord.

The sun set a rapid course for a horizon tinged in the color of autumn and chilled by that October fall. The path drifted into the chilled shadows of fall, the leaves having ceased their romp. The day's advance marked far more than the closing of a simple day. For the first time and the last time in my life it marked the closing of my mother's life as well. She seemed tied to this day, passing as it would pass. She was moving out of reach as was the sun and the day it defined.

Oddly, I had no alternative but to surrender. I fought the only option presented to me for an option that I did not have. A few of autumn's leaves swirled at my feet, dancing it seemed on this line between life and death, inviting me to race. They pirouetted as some grand waltz between life and death as if this place marked celebration, seemingly understanding the permanence of Mom's transition. The words "nevertheless, not as I will, but as thou wilt" (Matthew 26:39 ASV) seemed so easy for Jesus to say. The seasons seemed to grasp them. However, they were not easy, but Jesus said them anyway. I struggled to do so, for in doing so I released that which I did not hold. I stepped back. In the stepping I let go of that which I didn't hold, and I let my mother draw across that path and out of reach.

Tears once again mottled the surface of a gentle path that brushed the edge of a dense forest. The leaves raced off the edge of fall, and I found myself unexplainably able to release them to the next season. Although it was a fight, in the slow release I sensed a pending space to begin grieving. I cried in the fight against myself and the first thin wave of grief that the fight permitted.

CHAPTER 3

Closure—Fighting Against Ourselves: Releasing as Freedom to Grieve

Think not disdainfully of death, but look on it with favor; for even death is one of the things that Nature wills.
—Marcus Aurelius Antoninus

THEY LEAVE SPORADICALLY. SOME OF them go at the first hint of fall's advance. Others hang around until the first snows herd them southward as a rancher with heavy-footed cattle lumbering across pasturelands, gorged on the last of summer's grasses. The air is sullen and stilled by their absence, the void of song leaving a hole wide and gray. Trees stand as tenements emptied, their residents having taken wing for warmer skies.

But it was the geese really. Their movement was monumental, indescribably massive in scope as if a whole nation of waterfowl moved in unison. Other birds would cluster in sordid bands and bounce southward, a grouping here and a grouping there. But geese ... they would advance as an innumerable army seizing the very skies themselves.

As a kid, they would surge down the Atlantic flyway as if it were a conduit that compressed untold millions of geese into an invisible highway in the sky. The main body would come in droves of thousands, an endless string of black pearl strands being pulled southward, waving like the tail of a grand kite in the wind. It was too vast to embrace, being one of those things in life that defies the parameters of our imaginations and spills far outside the reach of our senses. Because it does, we're never quite done with it because we never quite absorb it all. It slips by experienced as something grand, but we inherently know that the grandeur that we were able to embrace was but a miniscule part of the whole. As I kid, I knew that.

The Atlantic flyway cuts a mystical swath through the heart of the southern Lake Erie region. All but an hour's drive or so away from home, we would tumble into the car and head out to sit on the sidelines of the miraculous. From miles away, you could see thin layers of black string formations low-slung across the sky, birds ascending and descending in numbers too vast to count. The water, the adjacent fields, the roads themselves were thick with them, each seeming to be an exact replica of the other, each energized with a corporate sense that something grand was afoot that was as individual as it was collective.

Even as a kid I knew that what I was observing was but a moment in time. Some things are too grand to last for long because you can only absorb so much wonder and majesty before you'll explode. But therein lies the rub. You want it to last, even if the sheer pleasure of it all kills you. At least death would be happy. You'd die with a smile.

To appreciate most things, you have to let them go. Some things become even more precious by their absence. When you lose something, you grieve the loss, and the exercise of grief can be brutally hard. At the same time, appreciation for that thing is dramatically enhanced in kind of a give and take exchange. It's the push and pull of life that as a kid watching a million geese I didn't get. All I wanted to do was to stand in the middle of this ocean of airborne life and somehow try to be a part of it, to find my place in it and believe that I could join it if only in the celebration of a season turning and a migration transpiring.

In feathered constellations of hundreds and sometimes thousands they would launch themselves from all around me in a deafening burst of pounding wings and haunting voices, assailing the sky and rising to warmer horizons. And in it I was left behind, simultaneously feeling a sense of abandonment, an equally thick sense of loss, but a deeper instinctual sense that this was right and proper and good. I had to let go. I had to let it be. I had to close out this moment, let it pass into my history, go home, and resume my life. As a kid, that was tough.

Yet there was something temporal in the grandness of it all. Jacques Deval said, "God loved the birds and invented trees. Man loved the birds and invented cages." Some things cannot be bound over or held, despite our desire to do so. It's in the context of unabated freedom that we experience the highest exhilaration and seize the fullest manifestation of that which we are enjoying. Caging it kills it because it robs life of the freedom to be its fullest self. Geese need to fly unfettered, otherwise the majesty is gone. Life is much the same.

Somehow making something temporal makes it precious. Standing amidst thousands of migratory geese, I knew that part of the magic lay in the fact that this incredible phenomenon was only momentary—a brief moment at that. Holding it would make it ordinary. I couldn't fathom it all as being anything but wildly extraordinary and so I stood in the midst of the sheer magic of the temporal and relished it until it passed. Then I would walk away with a living piece of the magic embedded in the heart of my soul. I had to allow it closure or the magic would be stripped.

Closure—Fighting Against Ourselves in Adulthood

Fall was passing, hugging the calendar on the cusp of an arriving winter that was set to push fall off the page. Sometimes life moves too fast. At times we want it that way. At other times we wish that the calendar would seize up and come to a complete halt, taking away the reality of a pending end and suspending change that we don't want. Why is it that we can't stop the clock even when it feels completely legitimate to do so? Why is time so ruthless and insensitive as to not grant us even the slightest pause—to hold the sweeping second hand of life for even a single moment when such a reprieve would allow us to briefly hold a little longer that which life itself is stealing away? To let kids stand amidst wild geese a bit longer?

But time moves on, creating an endless space within which change unfolds and flourishes. The passing of time means that all is in transition all the time. It means that we gain and lose along the way as part of the transition, but it also means that life always has the opportunity to be new, to be fresh, and to be tried again. It means that life is left wide enough and unfettered enough to unfold with all the boldness and mystical expansiveness that makes life, life. But with the freedom comes the reality of change and the fact that it renders everything temporary and existent only for a season. An end will come.

However, we can know that change and any end is grounded in "Jesus Christ [who] is the same yesterday and to-day, yea and for ever" (Hebrews 13:8 ASV). With that undergirding, we can find peace in change, knowing that change is ultimately grounded in Him Who is unchangeable. Therefore, change need not be feared, grieved, or hated as something that steals or depletes or cheats, but rather as something that is ordered by Him Who ordered the entirety of creation from eternity past and beyond. We can let change be the creative molder of life, hating it at times but believing in a final outcome as purposeful.

Passing and Change

Ice had begun to take a toehold around the edges of the pond. From the edges, it sent slight crystal fingers out onto the surface of water chilled and sullen. Songbirds had taken flight southward. Geese were massing in thread-like V-formations that drew silky black threads of pounding wings across graying skies, their call drifting in the deep woods as they passed. That year I had not stood among them. I had not for years.

Frost had laid a wafer-thin layer of ice crystals on the beams of the wooden bridge. It was yet tentative, instantly melting to the touch and pooling in tiny droplets under my fingertips. Everything was changing and I found myself angry and resistant about it all. I didn't care about what might be diminished in stealing freedom. I wanted life caged and held.

The Illusion of Holding What We Can't

I'm sometimes not ready for things to pass, for geese to ascend and cross horizons out of my line of sight. Life is precious. That which is precious we strive to hold. There is something about its value that drives us to possess it, to retain it; somehow feeling that possession is the only means by which that which is precious can be truly enjoyed. Without possession it is fleeting, easily escaping our grasp and robbing us of the pleasure that it brings. And so we seek out that which is precious. We hoard it if possible. We lock it up, insure it, put it in wills so that it remains under our control even in death, and do our level best to preserve it against anything that would steal it away. And because we hold it, it is no longer precious, for we have robbed it of what is most precious—the possession of inherent traits too precious to ever be held.

Yet, I think we hold the precious out of fear. Fear that life will be flat, that we will have lived empty lives filled with the damp grayness of a sullen existence, the kind of dampness that goes right through you and the kind of grayness that suffocates you. We fear that endings won't beget beginnings and that geese won't return. We have to accumulate that which is precious and keep it in order to stave off the dampness and lighten the grayness. But how do you possibly accumulate and hold a million geese heading south or a mother dying?

Life then becomes the summation of the possessions that we think we hold, which in reality is finitely very little, temporal at best, and killed by the fact that we're holding it. Our purpose becomes the continued holding of these things. It becomes our identity, whatever it is that these possessions are. Our passion becomes their maintenance so as to preserve them. Our hope becomes entangled in the continued accumulation of them to stave off potential loss. Our future becomes a cycle of maintenance and continued accumulation. And we can't let go because if we do, we'll have nothing left. We then lose the sense of awe when life sweeps our way, and we forfeit the humbling sense of appreciation when its time in our lives is concluded.

The Obedient Letting Go

"If you grasp and cling to life on your terms, you'll lose it, but if you let that life go, you'll get life on God's terms" (Luke 17:33 The Message). Fall was obediently letting go, not demanding some other terms. Summer had let go a long time ago, releasing all of the energy, vitality, and splendor of life despite the fact that the life it was releasing surged with a stamina and passion that simply seizes you with wonderment. Yet, summer let it go. Fall was letting go a spectacular inferno of color that raced through endless treetops and splashed the forest canopy to the sky's edge. It launched millions of geese and hurled them southward over forests thick with fall's fire. It was all precious and blindingly glorious, but life found a way to let it go, to release it, to allow it to be free. It seemed to celebrate and revel in the releasing as much as it did when the season first came.

Mom was dying, and I didn't want it to happen. I railed against letting go. I had no interest in closure because I didn't want the loss in the first place. She was precious beyond description, a woman unique in a way that makes uniqueness priceless. Time would not stop for her. The sweeping second hand moved with terrible precision, marking off precious seconds that I could neither hold nor halt. It seemed at that moment that I could hold nothing, precious or otherwise. Everything was slipping through my fingers and drifting off on the winds of time much like vapor caught in the swell of a firm breeze, much like geese rising and heading south without me.

We walked across the broad timbers of the arching bridge, into the hospice, and down the hall to her room. She was in the throes of death, able to hear but not able to respond. Pasty and a million miles drawn away from me, she lay there, each breath laborious and slow. Her eyes fell into a sinkhole of graying cavities, the blue sparkle having lost its luster as the light of her eyes faded and then found itself doused. Her vision had shifted, catching fantastic glimpses of something majestically eternal which only the eyes of her soul could see. It was all spectacular, rendering entirely unnecessary any need she might have for closure as the magnitude of her destination obliterated all loss. Those deep blue eyes were needed no more.

Obedience and denial found their place in me at the same time, each vying for a place that they could not simultaneously possess. I wanted to let her go but denied that I needed to. I was appalled by the course that freedom had chosen that was allowing her to die. I wished to hold her captive as I might hold endless hoards of migratory geese, not understanding the futility and absolute absurdity of such a thought.

For the next six hours every thought, each memory, the vast storehouse of emotions, the swill and swell of all that makes me human—all were plumbed to depths I could not have imagined. The more she faded, the deeper I went. Up from their subterraneous caverns all of these things surged in an engulfing flood, allowing me to touch my own humanity in a way that made my humanity entirely unfamiliar to me. I shared it with her as she drew further to some distant horizon that I could not go to, reciting those kinds of memories that sweep you away with warm and thick emotion regardless of the number of times you tell them or play them off the folds of your mind and heart. I surrendered to the inevitable course of life and watched her take wing as I had done as a kid engulfed in a million geese all gloriously free.

The Freshness of Obedience

And here I let go. I let go because life is not based on the holding of anything. Life is based on freeing yourself from holding so that you can embrace the wildness of the journey. Holding on to something renders you captive to wherever that thing is, holding you hostage to whatever that place is. Life that is held is life stagnant. Life that is stagnant is not life.

Life rolls on because it must, because it was designed that way. It's ever fresh, building upon the past in the present in order to enrich the future. Holding life kills it, much like holding a flower eventually wilts it. That which is precious can't be held or possessed because it's fragile and elusive. It's those qualities that make something precious. If it's not fragile and elusive, it's not precious.

So I let Mom go in a sheer act of will that seemed to entail more energy than a million geese aloft, with an exhilaration of equal proportions. I released her to a deepened belief that God's plan is a process, a series of events that flow much like a river, pooling here and there at times and cascading in a bubbling froth at others, but always moving. If we attempt to throw a dam across this river, it will pool, stagnate, and go no farther than the parameters of the dam we have constructed around it. It will eventually mass itself and burst any dam that we can construct because life is irreparably bound to achieve the complete manifestation of its design and intent. Freedom is entirely and indisputably indispensable to that objective.

Regardless, we attempt to manage it anyway. And in doing so, we will have managed it to death and controlled the vitality right out of it, much in the same way that forbidding the migration of geese would rob us of the wonder of it all. As if we could forbid it at all anyway.

Likewise, if I hold the past, I cannot simultaneously seize the future. My grasp will be directed in one place or the other, my energies vested in holding on to misty mementos locked in an unalterable past. Or I can take a firm hold of a future that is unwritten and therefore entirely unencumbered. Letting go lets me grieve. Letting go allows me to run in the natural currents of life, therefore resting in the fact that whatever the outcome, it will be good and right.

Grieving Through Accepting

At that moment, I began to grieve. Something broke open that permitted the first feelings of grieving to flow. You have to release to grieve. Releasing is accepting the course of things out of the belief that there exists a sure and certain order to this course. Geese fly south with an uncompromised certainty. Releasing releases us from our battle to alter the course that our life is taking, and to rest in both the gains and losses of where it's going: geese moving on, seasons turning, and Mom dying. We are free to celebrate wildly when it's called for. And we are likewise free to grieve deeply when it's appropriate. We can embrace both sides of life rather than attempting to control it in a manner that we experience neither.

A fall sun was preparing for an early slumber. A myriad array of geese and ducks had settled on the periphery of the pond, drawing up against the deepening twilight. I was once again able to walk among them, to join them a bit before I would lose them to the instinct of migration.

Mom would not live to see the next day. She would be gone by the time this array of waterfowl would take to the sky on pounding wings at the first blush of tepid dawn, heeding a call to skies far south. The sun would edge over the eastern horizon without her smile to illumine or her eyes to take in the glistening promise of a new day. For the first time in my life, the sun would rise without her. Life had moved on, leaving yesterday forever in a myriad collection of seemingly endless yesterdays. For the first time, she had moved into yesterday as well.

Acceptance—The Key to Freedom

Acceptance is our willingness to admit that we can't control life or direct outcomes. It embraces the fact that robbing life of the freedom it needs in order to be everything it was designed and ordained to be is deadly, audacious, and in the end entirely impossible anyway. Acceptance comes either as we teeter on the precipice of sheer exhaustion, our own spent nature leaving us no alternative, or as we readily embrace acceptance because it puts us seamlessly in step with God rather than grating against Him by vying for control with Him.

Acceptance is errantly viewed as surrender when it's really an acknowledgement that we don't have the control that we pretend to have and that we're not as powerful as we might like to think. Geese will fly and people will die. Acceptance is embracing our insecurities. It's recognizing that control is our attempt to establish a sense of security and safety in a frequently tumultuous world. Acceptance, then, is embraced by relinquishing our need to control and choosing instead to rest fully in God's constant care and provision.

That sense of acceptance that is heavy with peace and rich with empowerment is a sense that when walking with God, life rolls on as it should, even when the gravity of situations or their course would seem to suggest otherwise. It's about discerning the ebb and flow of life for the clues that God has placed there, rather than merely having our vision halted by questions about whether life is good or bad, fair or unfair, just or unjust. "Those who hope in me will not be disappointed" (Isaiah 49:23 NIV), says the God of geese and the overseer of death.

It's looking past the nature of events to the lessons and flecks of gold that God has scattered liberally within them. Acceptance is letting freedom give life ample space to do its work without our mindless intrusions and savoring its subsequent bounty.

We can accept whatever comes our way if we know that in the event, regardless of the nature of the event, God has placed something there for us that's of more value than the situation within which God has allowed it to come. Acceptance creates infinite room for an infinite God to work out the infinite in the finiteness of our worlds. It geometrically expands our worlds beyond the most unimaginable horizons. It breathes possibilities into everything that looms impossible. We throw open the windows of our existence, pulling back drapes of despair, and we let our souls air out in a vastness that takes our breath away. In the releasing that acceptance demands, we lose everything that we thought was something, and we gain everything that is truly everything.

As I kissed a dying forehead that was even now becoming cool, my hands stroked her face and brushed back hair so gray and still that it seemed to have already fallen into an eternal slumber ahead of my mother. A final goodbye. We stepped out into a parking lot somehow sterile and lifeless; people coming and going as if moving through some sort of mechanized script. The angst of holding on and letting go plied hearts and hands as they stood somber over awaiting cars, numbed and lost, fumbling for keys and answers.

And then they burst across the treetops. Hundreds of geese in a collection of V-formations surged over us, skimming the underside of a fall sky and brushing the last pastels of twilight. Fall accepted its own departure, seeing itself as part of some grand drama that played out in the simplicity of geese aloft or the vastness of a turning cosmos. Everything seemed thrilled to be a privileged part of it all. In embracing such a feeling, I found the beginnings of closure and a door to the future.

I waved goodbye to the airborne minions, and I said goodbye to Mom. Somehow in the letting go I experienced a transition to a place where I was allowed to settle: a place warm and familiar. And in this place of solace, I was likewise prepared for yet another unexpected goodbye.

CHAPTER 4

God as My Front Porch:
A Sure Place of Solace in Loss

Jehovah is my rock, and my fortress, and my deliverer; my God, my rock, in whom I will take refuge; my shield, and the horn of my salvation, my high tower.
—Psalm 18:2 (ASV)

THE FRONT PORCH WAS THE door to the world "out there." As a kid, it was the stepping off point to the world that never forced us to step off. It was the place through which the outside world would come into mine, monitored and managed in a way that didn't make the world safe, but that pared and neutered it sufficiently to make it safe whenever it was granted entrance. As a kid, other than it being huge, I didn't know everything that was out beyond the oak planks and cement steps. What I knew, however, was that the front porch would unflinchingly manage its entrance into my life.

It was a rarely used place because I found the solace of home much better than the turmoil of a world I didn't understand. The front porch was that first step out into that world, the threshold to whatever was out there. I suppose it was something akin to witnessing terribly frightening realities from a vantage point of absolute safety, vulnerability rendered neutral by either safety or the sturdy knowledge that safety breached would not be unsafe at all on the porch.

That's what made it the safest place of all. It was the stepping-off point to a big world that I knew little of. It seemed like the portal from the safety and embracing warmth of my world to whatever lay out there, fixed and firm but never naïve. In the child of my mind, the front porch edged right up to the world, but it held me perfectly safe and completely secure all the while. It provided me a front row seat as the happiness and horror of life paraded by, holding me, it seemed, entirely in perfect peace. I loved the front porch.

George Moore astutely pointed out that "a man travels the world over in search of what he needs and returns home to find it." Somehow I knew that I would someday step off the front porch and go out there into whatever the world was, and that the journey would eventually return me to this place. But for now, it was a magical and certain haven on the sidelines of life.

Fall always graced the front porch with vibrantly colored leaves from the massive maples that lined the street as mammoth sentries. Hardwood behemoths, they would rain color, drops of searing reds falling in torrents when the wind blew firm. Blown onto the front porch, they spun in royal red eddies, dancing with abandon as the wind courted them with a mix of tease and intention.

The turn of the season always invited me to the front porch to watch fall hand itself off to winter. You could watch it all safe-ly from the front porch, as you could watch anything. It was, it seemed, somehow the best of all worlds.

With three or four bulbous pumpkins, several stalks of dried corn cinched tight with flax cords, a ragged bale of hay, and a handful of incandescent leaves as trimming, we would dress the front porch for fall. It became a stage of sorts from which we would celebrate the departure of fall, pulling onto the front porch all the assorted things that symbolized the season. It was all staged right there on the oak tongue and groove flooring. We said good-bye from the safety of that place, acknowledging a passing from the kind distance that the front porch afforded us.

Adulthood and Distance Gone

There were other dying eyes the weekend my mom died, one pair so much younger and entirely unexpected. I met them on the front porch. It's not a long front porch, other than being long with the kind of miles that memories pave, lined generously with so much of my childhood. If memories were to define its breadth, it would stretch beyond any home to contain it. The tongue and groove flooring is yet firm, having welcomed and ushered feet both wandering and intentional to a sturdy oak door for nearly one hundred years. Friends, visitors, and strangers have all crossed its planking in order to engage the family within—that defining portal to the world out there.

How do you grasp a place framed by towering pines and muscular maples whose width and breadth hem you in above and around? Beyond the reach of their canopies, a sweeping lawn paints a tender, green expanse mottled with the glory of fall scattered about in leaves of gold, explosive red, and scintillating orange. Out past the fringes of its grassy mantle stand more forest behemoths that seem to challenge the enormity of the sky itself. The old porch is surrounded by a mantle of nature's best.

How do you engage a place that sits back just far enough from a sleepy street to muse as the world goes by while finding ample space between you and it? What do you do with hedges, thickets, and sweeping canopies thick with the chatter and chorus of birds singing out of the sheer rapture of living? What do you do with squirrels that skirt precariously on thin limbs as if taking no notice of the peril they place themselves at, leaping vast expanses of air from one forest behemoth to another? What do you do when life affords you just such a place?

But what do you do with it when you've engaged the sordid world out there in ways entirely unimagined by the childlike mind that staged fall on its expanse? What do you do when it seems no longer a portal because you've stepped out so far beyond it that you can never again step back to the other side of it, even when in your most dire moments you desperately wish that you could do so? What do you do with something that provided the most gracious and sacrificial protection imaginable but whose role seems to have been long terminated by time, circumstance, and this mysterious thing we call adulthood? What do you do?

If something this grand and yet this quiet is afforded you, then I would presume that you needed it. If you don't think that you needed it, there's a good chance that you're oblivious to your own needs or you're oblivious to the provision God affords us in our times of need. David sings, "Jehovah is my rock, and my fortress, and my deliverer; my God, my rock, in whom I will take refuge" (Psalm 18:2 ASV). Weave the metaphors and realities of our rock, fortress, and deliverer together and we have an impenetrable place of deep and certain refuge. We all need such a place for such times as those that were about to befall me. We need a front porch.

Permanent Provision for Grief

Is there always a front porch of some sort or other? Can there be a consistent place of unexplainable solitude that provides us a place of refuge? Can God carve out this kind of oasis in the midst of the most searing grief, an oasis that does not remove us from our grief but gives us complete sanctuary in it, that lets life move and circle all around us but provides us tranquility in it? More than that, do we need a place of such solitude and security that allows us to invite grief right into the middle of it, knowing that this place is so secure that nothing can shake it even when it is invited into the heart of it? Is that possible?

"I am with you always . . . ." (Matthew 28:20 ASV). "God is our refuge and strength, a very present help in trouble" (Psalm 46:1 ASV). We may find great relief and inexplicable solace in purposefully looking beyond grief in the midst of our grief in order to determine the provision made within it. Grief is consuming, wrestling away the sum total of our attention and energies in order to deal with it and attempt to flee from it. If grief becomes our focus, the hand of God is something other than our focus.

We don't think to look for any provision, as grief assumes none. Grief assumes a process by which grief is navigated and resolved, a process which rarely assumes a place from which to do it. Grief renders us vulnerable, which leaves us with the assumption that the struggle is ours alone. Grief calls us out. It strips us naked. It renders us helpless in our helplessness. It assumes little else and it does little else. Yet, what kind of front porch has God given us in the midst of our grief?

Loss Strikes Twice

Into it all, Paul walked onto my front porch and into my life again. He had walked into my life some thirty-five years earlier as a dear childhood friend, settling into my developmental years, navigating the tumultuous journey of adolescence alongside me until I left home for whatever it is that calls young men outward and sometimes upward. However, the demands of living and the scurrying about that seems so much wasted energy had long ago drawn us apart. He had changed over the gaping hole of the twenty-six years since we last said goodbye. The Paul that I knew was gone but there all at the same time. After over two and a half decades of unforgivable separation, Paul came by to visit.

Sitting there on that same front porch, we shared the passing of time and events, of life unfolding for each of us mostly in ways unexpected; the unanticipated and circular journey that led us from that front porch and back again decades later.

Trials and successes, painful failures and lost relationships, dreams realized and other dreams that we surrendered to the cold hands of reality. We talked about life through the eyes of middle age when the ever-increasing distance from the past rolls dim off some subconscious horizon of our minds, while the shortening days of the end of it all draws ever sharper. It was all amazingly rich. In a few moments, the years seemed erased.

With the friendship rejoined, Paul gazed into my eyes with a thick pause wrapped in an unexplainable intensity. With a frankness that belied the length of his own struggle, he cast a longing glance at the hearty trees that surrounded the front porch, ran his finger around the ring of his coffee cup, drew a breath of sweet fall air, and muttered that he was dying. It was not some sort of speculation that there might be a cure or that the treatment might yet stop the advance of cancer that relentlessly pushed forward on multiple fronts throughout his body. It was the surrender of a valiant warrior who felt that the battle might not be fighting cancer but closing out a middle-aged life in front of an audience of friends and family as a man of integrity, faith, and bravery. It was not about survival anymore, but about legacy.

His condition was terminal. Terminal is such a final word. It's the ultimate period that's put at the end of the last sentence on the final page of the book. Nothing follows it other than noth-ingness. Its finality is so unfathomable that you have no alternative except to hope that it really might have been mistaken for a comma, that it's some other sort of punctuation about the person's life that might legitimately suggest a pause before moving on again. But terminal . . . how I wished it was something other than the chilling finality of a period.

My mind instantly teetered, tipped in the emotional imbalance, and then plummeted. Whirling in wild gyrations, Paul's face immediately blurred and spun. A thousand memories, variant clips, and fragmented mementos of our shared childhood raced across the forefront of my mind at speeds that were emotionally deafening. My heart dropped so far that I had no sense of it any longer. An emotional paralysis humanly halted it all.

And then Paul's voice, soft and firm, grounded me. He said, "You don't need to say anything. Just thanks for listening and thanks for the years we had." The words, so needed, were wrapped in a silken veneer of complete peace that gently wrapped itself around me.

My mother was hours from death; Paul was two months or so away from the same thing. I bore both on that front porch. Stunned and pummeled twice. Blackness had fallen once, and then once again. Sometimes you are convinced that life has struck you sufficiently for it seems that its task in irrefutably crushing hope and driving you into some sort of trackless abyss has been so thorough that there is nothing left to destroy or maim. But sometimes life strikes twice, insanely attempting to kill that which has already been killed, finding some savage and sadistic pleasure in touting its victory and superiority by striking one more needless blow on its way back to wherever it came from. If life doesn't make sense, it's at times like these.

Being Truly Lost

Struck with a deafening blow by the pending passing of my mother and sent reeling again by Paul's disclosure, I was dead-center in that place: ground zero in grief. In those places there is no sense of bearing, of true north to at least know where you are. Most of the time when we talk about being lost, we have some general sense of direction that provides us a place to start heading off to. We at least have some vague and diffused sense of where to go.

But being truly lost is nothing of the sort. It's having absolutely no idea of where you are because where you are is a place you've never been before and could never have believed existed except for the fact that you're now there. It's having no idea where you should go because all that was once familiar is now terrifyingly unfamiliar and entirely uncertain, rendering the place that you need to go to as unknown.

All of this takes on the horror of a rapidly escalating panic as we suddenly realize that we are utterly and irrevocably alone in it all. Life at its worst isolates us because the more devastating it is, the more unique our experience in it. We become abjectly alone— that's lost. It is a rare, horrible, and deathly place that engulfed me on the front porch that day.

A Path Out of Being Lost

It was all too much, had I not borne the immensity of this while sitting on that front porch, that place of deep solace wrapped in majestic trees and God's thick arms. The front porch offered me a place of solace to watch two people that I loved embrace the reality of a world that is turning and turning dramatically. Oddly and unexpectedly, it was in the watching that I began to find my way out of the lostness.

Both were dying with great grace and valor. There was nothing of surrender in it at all. Surrender implies a weakness that renders us inadequate in conquering that which stands before us. Rather, death with honor and a chaste spirit was hardly weakness. It was bravery of the greatest sort. And on that front porch, surrounded by this place of refuge that God had granted me, I could see it all with great clarity and conviction.

It was not about searching for some path out of the lostness. It was all about watching. The keys and the compass were handed to me in the very things that had thrust me out and down into the abyss that I had plummeted into. Pain frequently results in panic. Panic seeks an immediate resolution and remedy by whatever means that resolution and remedy can be achieved. Panic frequently leads to a flailing and an impulsivity that only deepens and constricts the darkness that wraps itself around us with long, constricting, and chilling fingers.

I watched Mom and Paul courageously course their way through the onset of death, deciding to face it head-on with defiance and daring. They had each embraced a posture of bravery and faith: seizing the inevitable, turning death on itself by celebrating and cheering past victories, and savoring the innumerable gifts life had lavished on them. It became a recitation of glories, gains, gifts, and deeply flowing gratitude. It was the most genuine celebration of life that I had ever witnessed. I could not grasp it and felt that if I were the one facing death that I would be absolutely nothing of what they were. It was joyous and marvelous, mixed into some sort of wild and terribly rare concoction that I had no right to sip, but was handed by the glassful nonetheless.

Virgil stated, "They can conquer who believe they can." Conquering for Mom and Paul was about seizing the apparent untimely arrival of death and choosing a posture of celebration and savoring. I confess my inability to grasp it all other than I know it to be real because I watched them grasp it. They seized it in a manner that not only ministered to them but ministered to others as well. They believed that they could conquer . . . and conquer they did.

It was in this that I instantly found my bearings, both where I was and where I desperately wanted to go. Lostness dissipated by simply watching. The birds seemed to hold their songs for a moment and the trees leaned ever so slightly as if to hear a heart grasp a profound reality. The porch provided me the place. The examples provided me both keys and compass.

In the end, those keys and that compass allowed me to find myself so thoroughly and center myself so precisely that my sense of myself was honed sharper than it had ever before been. It was nothing short of stunning and astounding.

God as My Front Porch

"My God—the high crag where I run for dear life, hiding behind the boulders, safe in the granite hideout; my mountaintop refuge . . . ." (2 Samuel 22:3 The Message). Carefully listen to the metaphors of safety and security that are richly interwoven in this verse. God is the place of perfect security. It's not that life can't reach us there. God is not a god of seclusion, sweeping us away from all harm and setting us far out of the reach of a world of pain and inexplicable circumstances. He is our refuge right in the middle of this kind of world. He is the place that grants us the place to be found and to find. He is our front porch.

God is that place of perfect security in perfect insecurity. He is that place surrounded by enduring beauty, filled with His marvels so that we might not forget all that is good in all that is wrong. He places us just far enough from the world to muse at it while being separate from it, to find a place from which to learn the lessons that we need to fearlessly engage it. In Him there is a quietness that doesn't deny the cries of a hurting world, but a quietness that keeps it all at just enough of a distance to grow in it but not be consumed by it.

"Before you know it, a sense of God's wholeness, everything coming together for good, will come and settle you down. It's wonderful what happens when Christ displaces worry at the center of your life" (Philippians 4:7 The Message). That can only happen in just such a place. In our grief, God affords us a place like that—a front porch. And this place is strong enough to weather all the grief that life can throw at us. It is entirely sufficient.

It's a place quiet enough, safe enough, and sufficiently spacious for the keys and compass that we need to be handed to us in a manner that we fully see them, fully embrace them, and allow them to fully impact our lives. The front porch is then a place of safety but also a place that creates enough space for the miraculous to have plenty of elbow room.

It is an odd, indescribable, nearly inscrutable thing to be able to feel the searing intensity of a life unraveling, and to feel it all in the midst of perfect security that affords me both a path out of my own lostness and an opportunity for amazing growth. That is what God affords us in our grief. It is a most marvelous thing indeed.

Paul took it all in stride. He smiled, laughed with a contentment at the life he had been able to live, glanced at the trees and vast expanse of lawn covered in fall's flaming bounty, and said, "It's been a good life . . . it really has." Dying fully at ease, that's what he was doing. He exemplified God's security in a way most marvelous. God in our grief—that's what I saw in him. I know it works because I saw it in Paul. Mom exemplified it all of her life. The front porch created a place safe enough and expansive enough to see it.

Because I saw it, I was released to release that which was being lost to me. I was unexplainably released to come alongside my losses and tearfully yet boldly escort those very losses to the next place.

CHAPTER 5

Kisses in Death:
Processing Grief by Escorting Our
Losses to the Next Place

Don't walk behind me, I may not lead. Don't walk in front of me, I may not follow. Just walk beside me and be my friend.
—Unknown

WE WOULD WAIT UNTIL THE last deep frost, giving the garden and the greenhouse the fullest breadth of the season. Spring, it seemed, was only moments ago, the sweet scent of warm soils still thick and commanding. When you're a kid, it's not the planting that's fun because you can see and manage all of that. It's the growing that's mysterious as seeds transform in the cloaked secrecy of the soil, emerging as something far different from what they were when they were planted.

But by fall they had grown, produced both fruit and flower in abundance, and had succumbed to both the hard work of a long summer and now the biting hands of fall's frost. Their work done and their energies spent, they would all now be uprooted as either withering plants or hardened stalks. For a kid, there was a finality to it all, not exactly morbid but something of grief and loss.

There's unexpected loss where we're shocked into grief, a seismic abruptness where the unanticipated onset of grief is exponentially complicated by the massive disorientation that besets us. Then there's the expected loss, much like the garden and greenhouse where you can see loss coming from a long way off, where you see it as natural and inevitable. Expected or unexpected, we are equally set at grief's door to do grief's work. The method of arrival might be different, but the process of grieving is largely the same.

Clearing the garden and the greenhouse was an acknowledgement that this season was irrefutably over and that the plants that found refuge in it were dying without remedy or recourse. We had planted with a cycle fully in mind, knowing that we would have to plant again next spring. It was an acknowledgement of birth, life, and death, a cyclical process whose sidelines afforded us ample space to watch but no room to intercede in order to alter or suspend the cycle. It was the stuff of partnership but nothing of the stuff of control. I was a kid watching the fullness of life play out splendidly in the greenhouse and then the garden but having no idea of both the grandeur and pain of it all.

"Mediocrity knows nothing higher than itself, but talent instantly recognizes genius," wrote Sir Arthur Conan Doyle. The cycle of planting, growing, and harvesting seemed all the stuff of incomprehensible genius to me. As a kid, I didn't know what mediocrity was because I naturally assumed that you always lived with a generous sense of abandon. I didn't know that there was anything else. It seemed that I was appropriately naive. Life had not yet tainted me with so many of the unnecessary cautions that eventually weave their variant threads into the choking fabric of mediocrity. And so, as a kid I saw genius.

I suppose that the bareness of it all was the hardest to take, the end where life had been exhausted and the productivity had passed in some final, satisfied gasp. The spent remains of that marvelous productivity as displayed in dried, stocked, limp vines and shriveled stems were all that lingered. It was the absence of life that left the garden a naked plot of now frigid dirt and the greenhouse desolate and abandoned, one a cemetery and the other a mausoleum it seemed. You know life will come again, but its absolute absence where it had once flourished created a clash between the sense that nothing could ever grow here again and the sense of knowing with the fullest assurance that it will and it would.

It seemed that there should be some sort of formality to all of this—a bidding farewell that somehow closes this season with a reverence. There always seemed some sort of joint camaraderie that demanded that the party left at the end of it all would bid the other a passionate yet respectful goodbye. It was not just about saying goodbye to the other, but it was acknowledging the journey itself.

Celebration of the camaraderie of the journey was sweet and tender, thanking both the garden and greenhouse for a journey well done and wonderful. It was recalling the myriad fruit and flower that had been a product of plants now exhausted and spent in the production. The focus was not on the remnants that remained, but celebrating the glories of what they had accomplished and what they had graced my life with over those sweet and lingering months of spring and summer.

Whether it was the greenhouse or the garden, we planted seeds in the bosoms of both and we tended them through the months. But it was the greenhouse and the garden that nurtured them and did with those seeds what we could not. We prepared a place for the magic of germination and growth, but we didn't perform it. That was the wonder and genius of the greenhouse and the garden. It was a marvelous partnership. This whole wondrous partnership and the fruit that it yielded brought celebration squarely into the heart of grief.

So in the fall, when the frost had closed the final chapter to the season, I would stand in the garden, run clumps of dirt through grieving fingers, and bid the garden goodbye. Tucked in with a thick, downy blanket of mulch ground from the mounds of fallen leaves shed by adjacent trees, the garden seemed to smile, roll over, and nod off to a winter's slumber.

In the greenhouse we would turn off the water, store the pots and planters, sweep the counters clean of any stray potting soil, lock the windows tight against winter's pending cold, and bid a second farewell. The greenhouse seemed more vigilant, holding its stores safe in its cinderblock and glass bosom until spring would prompt it to release it all in a celebration of seeds and sweet soil. It was almost an expression of affection at the end of a wonderful journey, escorting the garden and the greenhouse to the next season. It came every fall.

An Affectionate Goodbye in Adulthood

When the end comes, what do you do? How do you go about that final goodbye that's not about "goodbye until next time," but that's about "goodbye until the next life"? How do you say goodbye in a way that closes out your relationship in this life for the rest of this life?

We rarely extend a goodbye with that type of irreversible finality. The concept of goodbye has been woven heavy with a sense that a "hello" will follow in some short order. So a "goodbye" that has no such threads woven through it, whose tapestry is sewn with nothing but the threads of loss, is unknown and unwanted.

But is our role simply that of extending a goodbye and centering down to grieve the loss that we've sustained? When we speak that devastatingly final goodbye, is our role simply to deal with all the searing emotional shrapnel and rush to stop the rampant hemorrhaging that oozes our lifeblood out of places that we didn't even know existed? Or when it comes to loss do we have a greater, more profound role?

Darkness had fallen coal black and thick, swirling around the hospice as a dank fog drifting in from the shoals of nighttime. The colors of fall and the transition of the fiery season were hidden under a blanket of nighttime black that muted the colors and rendered them entirely cold. It was as if every drop of the lifeblood of fall had been mercilessly drawn out, rending fall the anemic pallor of blacks, dirty whites, and thin grays. Night had sucked the blood out of whatever bit of life the previous day had left. So stark was the absence of life that its presence was hard to visualize even though I had lived it and embraced it innumerable times. The turn of the day had hidden the turn of the season.

Nature moves on, adding and subtracting as it goes. It seems to welcome that which is born into it as readily as it releases that which dies. Nature turns in response to a far greater axis that spins the planet and sets both the solar system and the cosmos on clockwork journeys. The hand of the Creator sets creation itself to a cadence ultimately destined for destruction in this life so that all that is good might be gathered up and saved for eternity. All of that same grandness, wonder, and eventual loss was played out in the greenhouse and garden every year as a kid. It was about to play out in ways I could not have imagined.

On this night, nature seemed to stop in the transition, catching its breath so as not to miss the grand turn of seasons set on a course of rest and reprieve. The pond was kissed by a wafer-thin layer of ice that reflected the galaxies spinning light years above it. The moon had settled as a slice of pasty white in a dark sky riddled by stars, itself transitioning from a round orb through phases headed once again to fullness. Geese and various waterfowl had settled on quiet banks, heads tucked under downy wings. An owl, the lone harbinger of the night, called deep into sullen woods, its haunting and nearly cottony voice weaving through thick stands of hard-woods as if providing some element of warmth and life to it all.

The lights of the hospice shone golden against the chill out-side. It seemed to wrap the dying in a place both safe and rubbed warm so that they might embrace their passing in the greatest calm and security. All in its bosom seemed held in a protected embrace as the world looked on both sad and sadly expectant. It was much more than simply a place to die. It was a place that lovingly enveloped the dying, escorting them from one life to another with a mix of chivalry, honor, and respect. Dying was not a relinquishment, but a passing which involved a partnership.

The call had come in the night. Mom was passing. Her heart-beat had softened and her breathing drifted ever shallower. The final goodbye was racing toward us, framed and counted not in days or even hours, but in mere minutes. Minutes remain the same length whether they are held against the span of years or minutes themselves. Yet, when minutes are held against themselves, they seem so terribly brief. Minutes were all that was left.

The assemblage of minutes would not be sufficient for us to arrive in time. She would pass minutes before we stepped in the door. However, Dad had spent the night, recognizing this to likely be the last of over fifty years of nights with his wife.

Kisses in the Escorting

His own humility would preclude his ever disclosing his actions during those final minutes as they slipped by draped in sullen shadows both in the room and in his heart. The picture of Mom's passing was painted by a nurse who found something special in this moment. She had witnessed the passing of thousands, yet this turn of life unexpectedly pulled her heart tender and moved her to tears. In her own emotion, she drew us aside and etched with deep words those last moments, handing us in those few seconds a picture most remarkable.

Peering into the room during those last minutes, she saw Dad's hand lay on Mom's chest, wanting desperately to feel the last few beats, hoping to carry away with him something of the last of her life to add to the bounty of what had been lived with her. There was desperation borne of a heartfelt passion to grab even the slightest final thread to add one more facet to the massive tapestry woven over their fifty years together. The nurse said that his eyes never left her . . . not for the briefest moment. He gently kissed her on the forehead over and over, loving her out of this life and into the next, sending with her the unmistakable message of his love and undying devotion. Trembling hands pressed upon hers, and he loved her and prayed her into the Kingdom.

He did nothing out of greed or loss. There was no anger, no attention to the angst that ground his heart to parched powder. Inside he was dying right along with her while being left alive in his own emotional death to face life without her. There was no focus on any of these things. Neither did he pay attention to the horrendous loss that was raining into his life as an emotional downpour of torrential proportions. There was only the love of a simple man who escorted his wife into eternity in the finest, most unselfish manner that one can conceive: obediently handing her off to a God Who was calling her home while temporarily leaving Dad here.

It was all beautifully selfless. In the soft shadows, a husband released his wife with all the costs of doing so suffocating and simultaneously rocking a gentle heart. Dad let it be so. His total focus was on escorting a beloved wife to the edge of this life and allowing her to step over, leaving him on this side terribly alone.

He was graceful, selfless, and undying in his commitment to her. And in this grandest of all moments, I saw in my father the majesty of something eternal wrapped in the wonder of all that the human spirit is capable of. In him I saw the combination of what a man surrendered to God could be and could do. I watched him raise himself immeasurably above himself, take his wife by the hand, and selflessly escort her out of this life into the next one. Awe swept over me, humbling me and stunning me all at once. Once she was fully escorted out of this life and his task was completed, he turned, bent over, and cried.

Grieving in Escorting Our Losses

We grieve most effectively when we accept our loss and then boldly take the extra and terribly selfless step of escorting our losses out of our lives and into the next. Escorting our losses demands letting go of whatever was lost and forgoing the implications of that loss in order to set ourselves aside momentarily and escort that loss home. When faced with the enormity of such a task, it all seems impossibly impossible. It would even appear to border on the ridiculous. But it frames the grieving process at the very outset in ways that lay a precious and vital foundation for effective grieving and profound healing.

The concept of escorting our losses to the next place embraces and wholly joins in the natural transitions of life, but it demands a selflessness that is unrelenting and entirely uncompromising in its complete exclusion of greed. Greed gives us permission to be the victim. Assuming the victim role provides us a vehicle or manner in which to process and proceed through our losses as we make their focus much more about us and the specific impact of the loss to us and on us. Such a posture brings loss close to home, thereby putting it more fully in our control. It marginalizes loss, focusing it more specifically to us so that its scope is dramatically diminished and we can therefore contain it much more readily. It manages loss so that we can somehow survive it and walk away as unscathed as possible.

Conversely, escorting the losses out of our lives makes the process more about joining the natural, God-ordained transition of life and embracing the sovereignty of God. It is other-focused in the sense of larger life and God's overall plan. It means that I deal with my losses once I have escorted this person or this thing on to wherever it is they are naturally designed to go.

Grieving is more aggressively freed to happen when our posture is not one of focusing on our own losses or bemoaning the unfairness of life. It's in this very place that most of us get stuck. It's recognizing the turn of the seasons and releasing those things with a vigor that moves us to move them on.

There is in all of this a relinquishment that has a certain vigor to it. We join our God in His purposes by not only relinquishing the things that He is moving on, but assisting, even celebrating the moving. The partnership in God's grand design becomes our focus rather than the loss of whatever it is that God is bringing to a close. This doesn't necessarily take away our pain in the face of our losses. Nor does it mean that we are freed of the grieving process. Rather, it assists us in embracing purpose in our pain as well as meaning in our loss.

Seizing Our Role in Loss

Where are we focusing in our losses? Typically, it's on what we've lost, and all of our responses extend outward from there.

Loss becomes all about the loss, a consuming cycle that permits no movement beyond the loss. Because that's usually the case, it's all about things like unfairness, injustice, a life forever changed against our wills, questioning our choices, a misguided focus on recouping the loss, and all those kinds of things. Those things are all a natural and normal part of loss. Yet they afford no resolution in and of themselves.

It's taking that extra step of ushering our losses to wherever they are destined to go. There's a radical reorientation where we not only let go but also participate in moving our losses out and away from us. We embrace life as a journey where we and everything around us are always in transition. Sometimes life appears stable with the evidence of any sort of transition as entirely absent. Such a perspective is little more than our desire to wish life as stable and constant. Other than God, the only constant is change itself.

Effective grief embraces change. It grieves loss and it works against our natural inclination by moving that which is lost on to whatever or wherever it is intended to go. Dad ushered Mom into a life where we all have yet to go. He sent her ahead of himself at great cost to himself. He embraced the two-fold trauma of letting go and simultaneously escorting her home. That's the stuff of grief. It's embracing two entirely contradictory facets of our humanity: wanting to desperately hold on, yet letting go all the same.

There is that natural, terrible internal clash in loss where the very thing we're losing is the very thing we want to keep. Two opposing realities, each in their own right powerful enough to consume the sum total of our energies, vie for the exact same ground in our hearts at the very same time. The titanic clash dissolves our energies, exhausts our stamina, and suffocates hope with a horrifying totality.

The monumental struggle is bringing the passion to hold on in submission to the desire to let go. It seems the David and Goliath scenario, except we face it with no sling and no stones. It is won, however, in loving the thing being lost with such an inflamed passion that we desire to escort it on and out of our lives. We hold a love for it strong and deep enough to absolutely forbid that it exit life alone. We realize that if we try to hold it, we will fail and it will leave without us holding its hand, stroking its face, and kissing its forehead. We love the thing or the person enough to refuse to leave its last moments to both the hands of death and the terribly barren landscape of loneliness. When out of love we choose to be this selfless, we have the sling and the stones to do the impossible . . . to let go and escort our greatest loss with the greatest compassion.

Dag Hammarskjold wrote these words: "Pray that your loneliness may spur you into finding something to live for, great enough to die for." It would seem reasonable that escorting others out of this life creates a loneliness cutting enough but grand enough to give us something great enough to live for and die for.

It is the grand task and the grand sacrifice. It may end in loneliness, but a loneliness manifest of great sacrifice and something of infinite love. Such loneliness may be bitter, but it is borne of the raw manna of life. Remarkably, the loneliness of escort gives us something to live for and something great enough to die for. It gives loss room to bequeath a crowning touch on that which is lost and that which will pass into the night. In the wincingly sacrificial role of escort, the eyes of both heart and soul focus not on loss, but on everything the loss was and is yet to be when held perfect and fast in God's eternity. It makes space for something to come to a pinnacle so that we might celebrate it all the way to a marvelous closure.

CHAPTER 6

A Passing in the Night: Loss as the Crowning Touch

Fiery colors begin their yearly conquest of the hills, propelled by the autumn winds. Fall is the artist.
—Takayuki Ikkaku

THE KITCHEN WINDOW FRAMED EVERY morning all year long; lacey curtains provided a soft, nearly translucent matting for the promise of a new day. The wavy-glassed window with its spray of tiny encased bubbles had looked directly east, dead-center into the face of every morning for the nearly one hundred years that the house had steadfastly stood there. Between the kitchen window and an ascending sun there stood trees numerous and varied, a prolific profusion of forest and colossal canopies. On that particular morning, fall had burst their canopies into exploding flames of color.

Every fall, on some anointed morning the sun would rise entirely unobstructed by clouds or haze. For a few brilliant moments it would set the foliage ablaze, backlighting blood reds, throbbing oranges, and supercharged yellows with color that sent the senses hopelessly to the end of themselves. Some of the sun's rays would slip undetected through the treetops, emerging from the canopies and hedgerows as soft slices of transparent yellow. These would pool in tiny puddles of gold on the whisper-thin layer of frost that had blanketed the ground. The kitchen window framed the wonderful wildness of it all. As a kid, those mornings were stunning.

Sometimes in the mundane of daily life, there arises an entirely unexpected, completely exhilarating moment where everything instantaneously coalesces in an absolutely stunning moment. Somehow everything comes together all at once as if a million different rivers converged into one massive, surging torrent of life, where everything is present and alive and living in one single place for just a single monumental moment. In this coalescing, there's a pinnacle experience where life pulls the wonder of itself to some sort of wondrous peak.

John Calvin wrote, "Here on earth we may have a foretaste of the divine kindness, so that our hope and longing may be kindled for the full revelation of it." The mornings when fall peaked could have been nothing other than "a foretaste of the divine kindness," as nothing on earth either individual or assembled could account for it or possess enough of itself to reach such a pinnacle.

In the peaking of fall, it seemed that this dying, fallen planet somehow remembered its origins and reached just high enough to scratch the underside of heaven. In doing so, a scant few flecks, shards, and snippets of heaven itself seemed sufficiently jostled to slip out from the underside of that place. They descended with a formidable, effervescent power that was silently woven with heavenly laughter and thick with gracious intent.

By it and with it we were momentarily graced, being brushed by something we were not a part of but something that we were designed for. Those moments were a sweet foretaste of the most divine sort. Sometimes heaven shows up just long enough for us to catch a fleeting glimpse of it as we turn to catch sight of it. When earth is drawn into a grand culmination of whatever sort, it rises as at no other time. In doing so, it brushes the underside of heaven, allowing us to catch sight of heaven on earth. Such were those fall mornings.

Samuel Johnson wrote, "Let us consider the objects of our sight as leading us directly to Him who is invisible." Can the perfect culmination of fall be anything less than that? As a kid I never asked the question because I automatically assumed it to be so.

Sometimes the "all and everything" of life is drawn together as part of a grand summation that silently reminds us of the wonder of all that is. Life is suddenly framed in a glorious conclusion that a grand work is now completed. Something tediously crafted, laboriously nurtured, and tenderly aged reaches some sort of pinnacle that is brief but wildly glorious. Such moments are both celebration and loss, celebrating a work completed and recognizing that in the completion it is now time to move on.

Such was a brilliant fall morning out the kitchen window. There was about it all the sense that the seeds and fresh soils of spring, followed by the long nurture of a warm summer kissed by a generous sun, had reached their climax in the brilliance of a stellar fall morning. There was nothing to be added, as adding to something so perfect was impossible anyway. At these kinds of moments you can freely and therefore fully embrace the splendor lavishly arrayed before you simply because your mind isn't occupied with ways to make it better or touch it up because there is nothing to touch up. Perfection is perfection. You're left standing with but the one single option of bearing your soul to this pinnacle moment and letting it all course in.

Standing there as a child wild-eyed in wonder, you didn't want to touch any of it for fear it might be ruined. You had no sense that you could make it better, which kept me from trying to do exactly that. As a kid, there was something untouchable and complete about it all that invited nothing more and nothing less than reverent contemplation and riotous celebration. To pack those two things into a kid's body on a fall morning when the artistry of creation peaks and then cut him loose to somehow absorb it all was magic.

The frame of the kitchen window was simply too small to take it all in. Sometimes the windows we look out of are constructed just big enough to bring in sufficient light, but not nearly large enough to usher in glory. We live lives of small windows. Life reaches grand pinnacles before it brings the thing created to rest. When we face loss we frame our windows even tighter so as to minimize pain and reduce the scathing sense of loss. When we do that, we miss the grand finale that displays the marvel of the thing now coming to completion. We live lives of small windows, cheated of glory and bereft of grandeur unimaginable.

And so, gasping for more, I would run outside to watch it all without any kind of diminishing frame. In the backyard, fall would stretch itself from horizon to horizon, the sun easily engulfing it all and raining golden hilarity upon it all. It seemed a pinnacle of the year, so glorious yet so terribly reverent that you felt that you shouldn't have even been there. As Aaron Rose said, "In the right light, at the right time, everything is extraordinary." These mornings were extraordinarily extraordinary.

As I stood there in awe of it all, fall rendered an unexpected final touch of genius. Across the arch of the newborn morning, a flock of geese flew, plying the gold of the morning with a tenured sense of reverence, moving from the lake to feed in adjacent fields. Something of lofty grandeur, they skirted the treetops, their underbellies rendered golden by fall's brilliant and still fresh sunrise. It added life to the fire in the treetops, geese affirming this moment as a pinnacle now concluded, now free to head south. They drew away over forest, their calls being drawn through the woods, skirting the underbrush in an attempt to catch up with geese headed south. At all of this the artist seemed to sit back, smile, and enjoy the culmination of it all.

Fall was the final touch of a long year. The artist's brushes indeed seemed laid aside. Paints were stored and the canvas was celebrated as completed. Fall would only last a moment—a whisper-thin wonder in the span of eons. As a kid you wonder why it can't stay.

Why does something so perfect have to be so temporal? Why isn't it like this all the time? That's just it. Life brings things to a pinnacle, to a point of completion where this thing is finally all that it was meant to be, a wild expression of the manifold glories of this season condensed into a single, concentrated moment. In these moments, there is a celebration and a conclusion all at once. The sun lifted, the glory passed, and I prepared for the doldrums of school.

What Gets in the Way

We are of the mind that things can always be improved. Part of that mindset rests in an unconscious sense that if there's something yet to add, we don't have to let go just yet. Improvement rationalizes retention. Yet true living means understanding that at some point, additions only result in diminishments. At some point completion is inevitable but likewise frightening.

Completion means celebration of the things completed; but it equally means something is finalized. It concurrently means moving on to that which is next. Despite the celebration, moving on can be tough. So sometimes in life's journey it's not about improvement. Rather it's about completion, celebration, and then release. Our mindsets must move from the incessant mentality of tweaking and tucking and touching up to simply taking stock of something completed.

Completion in Adulthood

Darkness compounded darkness that night. Sometimes darkness seems layered upon darkness as life moves in and out of our lives. It would sometimes seem that loss did not happen in isolation. Rather, losses seemed joined together in some string of events that fed upon and compounded all the other losses. When that happens, loss becomes overwhelming.

The night sky had gone soft and sullen with woolen clouds, snuffing out a whole galaxy of stars. The moon had abandoned the night, leaving the sky vacant. Branches cracked in the chill of the night air, splintering the silence of a night fitfully asleep. It seemed that the night had swallowed any sense of time, suspending in limbo a season turning on an eon-old schedule. Something seemed out of sorts that night.

Mom had passed into the night and into eternity ten minutes before I returned to the hospice. She had slipped away, quietly and unobtrusively in the same way which she had lived her life. Never clamoring for attention, she served quietly. Once she had completed whatever the task might have been, she slipped into the background, allowing the other parties to sip and savor whatever delights she had left in her wake.

On this occasion, she slipped into the background forever, leaving a lifelong legacy of delights too numerous to recount and far too expansive to embrace. It seemed the final exit, with all having been left uncompromisingly completed. It was time.

When a painting is completed, adding or subtracting the most subtle touch can ruin the entire picture. Mom was a masterpiece completed, leaving even the minutest touches to diminish what she was. As with that fall morning as a child standing in a kitchen engulfed in the grand fury of fall, God deemed the masterpiece completed. The brushes were put down. The paints stored. The canvas held and admired. Mom was then framed with eternity.

Framing Loss

Is loss really loss, or is it the pinnacle of God's work in a person's life, much like fall? In a life well lived, is it really nothing more than an acknowledgement that the final touches have been made, that the person has been fully painted with the brushes of perfection? At these moments, would it not make sense that anything else, any addition despite how small, would only bring diminishment? Is it reasonable to believe that it's now time to frame that person or that situation with the timelessness of eternity, handing whoever or whatever it is over to God?

That night it was not just about loss. It was about completion. It seemed that Mom's life had been perfected and that the portrait that God had intended had been perfectly completed. Loss collided head-on with this sense of completion, leaving me standing over her stilled frame feeble and crying for whatever little bit more of her I could beg God to give me. Yet I knew her time, her place, and her impact were completed. The only thing left was to frame the magnificence of this woman in the frame of the eternal.

It was an irreconcilable moment of extreme contradictions, standing over the bed, now cradling the lifeless body of my mother, desperately wanting more time but fully satisfied with the sum total of her life. Begging for yet another conversation, one more hug, one final smile, or one more story of some foggy childhood memory, yet simultaneously knowing that it would only mar what had been brought to such perfection. It's the kind of contradiction that's entirely clear but completely muddled at the same time. The only way to grasp it is to move away in time and let the larger reality of God's work in her settle as muddied waters left alone eventually become clear and crystalline.

Managing Grand Contradictions

There are times when the magnitude of the human spirit is revealed with such wonder and ferocity that we are stunned as to God's creation within us. So grand is His genius that we can both feel and embrace powerful emotions of opposite proportions at the same time. We have within us the capacity to want to hold that which is inexplicably dear to us, while concurrently loving it so fully as to let it go.

Such opposites would seem to tear the very core of our souls, finding no habitable ground where the two could possibly coincide. Yet they do. It is when life demands the impossible that we have the God-given tenacity to step up and do the impossible. We can feel tremendous loss and long to hold that which we have lost while at the same time giving it permission to go. We need not stand in one single place in life, thinking we can only occupy one place and have one single experience at a time. Loss infuses us with the sense that we can live in many places and experience multiple experiences at one time. We are built to embrace the eternal diversity that defines creation itself. Loss invites us to do so and likewise forces us to do so.

As I bent over, kissed her cooling forehead, and stepped back from that deathly still bed, this ferocious dichotomy sent my knees weak. With all the fabric of a grieving heart I wanted her back, yet I knew that her life was completely complete. I felt that I would be entirely unable to walk out of the room. The door, a mere fifteen feet away, seemed miles removed. Glancing up at it, it seemed a small opening at the end of a long, dark corridor.

Then something meshed. There was a miraculous accommodation where holding and letting go found a common ground. Both accepted the other, finding in the expanse of my heart a proper place for each. It was normal to grieve and it was likewise normal to celebrate. Both fit despite the disparity between the two. Here I began letting go. The door seemed closer.

Trusting the Human Dichotomy

We engage life at a level determined largely by our perception of our abilities. Our point of reference is not who God created us to be, or the fact that we are made in His image and therefore possess some of His inherent vastness. The fact that we are sons and daughters of the living God in terms of both likeness as well as privilege is lost. We have forgotten who we are if indeed we ever really knew in the first place. Therefore, our conceptualization is based on purely human standards and perceptions that cheat us of a true understanding of the vastness of ourselves.

We draw thick lines around our lives and erect tall fences based on our limited perception of who we are. We perceive but a marginally thin slice of the whole, unaware of the vastness within us that lies undetected. We then manage life entirely based on the perceived resources, thereby cautiously calculating what we can do or be or tolerate based on this thinly marginalized view of ourselves. The lines then are tightly drawn and the fences are drawn in. The window frames are drawn tight and the world outside goes unnoticed and begging.

Sometimes, however, there is a merging where life comes at us full force. At those times something entirely unexpected and completely unknown rises up within us. We find ourselves sometimes suddenly and always dramatically standing beyond any preconceived line or limit that we had assumed for ourselves. "Yes, and he will show him even greater works than these, so that you will be amazed" (John 5:20 NIV). We do what we thought we were unable to do. At these moments the grand magnitude of our inherent humanity broaches who we thought ourselves to be, rendering us much larger.

At those moments we realize, at least for that moment, that we can do that which we thought ourselves unable to do. The incomprehensible becomes comprehensible. The impossible finds itself pulled within the realm of the possible. Fear is surmounted and pain is contained. We can stand at the various bedsides in life and simultaneously hold on and let go in the very same instance.

Our Humanity and God's Infinity

In these times we dramatically rise beyond ourselves as we connect with the vastness of our own humanity and fuse that humanity to an infinite God. We are then thrust to levels and places that we thought insurmountable and entirely unattainable. We are more than we perceived ourselves to be, standing as we were designed to stand but entirely unfamiliar with the design that allows us to stand there. At those times we are beset with wonder and confusion all at once.

Standing beside Mom's deathbed, I found the self that God had created and endowed with His character. I did what I could never have imagined. The horror of loss screaming from the cooling body of my mother should have thrown me into the panic of denial. But I became more. I became someone who in that instant desperately wanted it all to be an unwanted nightmare, but I concurrently embraced it and let it go. The two sides of holding on and letting go found equal room within my heart, yet they found a supernatural balance. I walked out of that room in peace. I should have not been able to do that, but I did. And that peace stayed for the years that followed.

We are more than we perceive ourselves to be. Our capabilities are incomprehensible and magnificent. They exist only because we are crafted and born in the image of an infinite God, holding within us shards and semblances of His inexhaustible and wholly indefinable character. When we take our humanity and join it to this infinite God, the possibilities are limitless, the capabilities are fathomless, and the opportunities are endless. Whatever bedside we stand beside and whatever loss that bedside entails for us, we can let it pass with a sense of profound victory.

Loss then presents us with the opportunity to discover who it is that we are. It forces us outside our constricted parameters and the small windows that we huddle behind, and it thrusts us out into everything that we are but never dared to be. Loss is the fertilizer of growth, spread broadly and liberally. It brings to our lives the power of growth in ways that nothing else does or can. Loss is so much more than loss.

Despite the inherent pain, loss is about growth both magnificent and unimaginable. It is so powerful that it brings growth even when the sun doesn't rise. When all is dark and cold and foreboding, loss overcomes and brings growth even when it is far too dark to see it or apprehend it. God works in the dark to display us in the light, and those pinnacle moments find their origins in those very places.

CHAPTER 7

A Sunrise That Didn't: Expanding Our View of Life

If winter is slumber and spring is birth, and summer is life, then autumn rounds out to be reflection. It's a time of year when the leaves are down and the harvest is in and the perennials are gone. Mother Earth just closed up the drapes on another year and it's time to reflect on what's come before.
—Mitchell Burgess

FALL CALLS FOR A CLOSING down. Life is stored until it can be unpackaged at spring's arrival. In the closing down there was also a narrowing of the world. Somehow things contracted as they were prepared to be held tight against an impending winter. In the summer, the embrace was as wide as life itself. In the winter, life wrapped its arms tight around its bosom in a closed embrace as a means both to keep itself warm and to give itself permission to rest. Fall was that preparation.

Storm windows did that. They held the outside on the outside. All summer long we begged summer in through screen windows that populated every room of the house. Summer drifted in softly in passively warm breezes that brought the caress of summer through every room. Its breath would fill the veneered curtains on its way in, expanding the chest of the fabric as if the curtains were inhaling a giant breath of summer. It would then press them against the screens on the way out, the curtains playing with the expanse of the season in the folds of their fabric, seemingly unwilling to let summer's breeze pass back outside.

Throughout the summer the outdoors was invited in, even coaxed in through a giant window fan that funneled summer into the heart of our house. Ample room was made for the vastness of summer itself to come inside and visit. And so it did, not as a commandeering presence, but as a warm and powerful giant that wanted nothing more than to rub us warm and fill the house with the sweetest of summer scents.

On its arms it ushered in the thick yet delicate aroma of lilacs. It swept in the sweet scent of tender summer rains and the sound of choruses of crickets and extended the night out to the farthest horizons to carry in the whistles of distant trains and a world enamored with living.

Summer came in through screen windows that begged summer to gather up all of its warm delights and to pass through with armloads of everything that made summer what it was. And pass through it did, coming in and then inviting us out to play with a brazen boldness that makes play nothing of work and everything of sheer, unadulterated pleasure.

But now, with the onset of fall, we set about to hang a myriad of glass windows that would no longer give the outside permission to come in. We could embrace summer, but we had to savor winter from a slight distance. When the storm windows were hung, the world shifted, closing in from seemingly endless horizons to the four walls of the old farmhouse.

As a kid, life seemed always open and endless. There was a horizonless adventure about it all, characters and lands of myth, legend, and imagination that spun my mind out to places mystical and endless. As a child, imagination unseated fear, entirely displacing it in the wild wonder of possibilities and experiences untried. There was something naively tenacious about being a kid: that the thirst for adventure and the unknown, of keeping the windows wide open, remained even when some event would suggest that you should throw up the storm windows and lock yourself tight against the world.

Nonetheless, something was lost when the storm windows went up. It was an acceptable loss as we prepared to take refuge against the razor-cold winds of winter. The pulling down and pulling in was accepted as a part of what we always did when fall fell on the landscape. What played bigger was the anticipation of taking the storm windows down on the other side of the calendar to invite summer in once again. But for now, the storm windows were hung and the world closed in.

Closing Down and In as an Adult

Sometimes it's dark even when it's light. Sometimes life is jolted in such a manner that it never realigns itself the same again. Sometimes a fog of sorts rolls in and when it pulls away its damp veil, it seems to have both added something and subtracted something. In the end, whatever the scenario, the landscape is forever changed, leaving what was as a memory and always a memory. Sometimes life closes down and it all looks different.

The morning of Mom's passing never came. The world has closed down to the degree that morning simply never came. My world had extended from horizon to horizon. Mom had taught us to live that way. Her example and her foundation gave us the confidence and tenacity to run the breadth of whatever horizon beckoned. She taught us that a vibrant faith in God made any horizon only as far away as we chose it to be. Horizons did not mark the end of what we could see, but the beginning of what we could not see. It was all the passion of adventure and our ability to embrace it. Suddenly, those horizons vanished, leaving no place for a sunrise that first day. It didn't happen.

Sometimes life irrevocably shifts, instantly taking a course that jettisons us out of our lives into something that is not our lives. We seem to pass through some sort of dimensional rift that is vapor-thin on one side, giving us no resistance when we are thrust through it. Once across, the way we passed in through seems now a steel door thick, sealed, and foreboding, allowing us no passage back to the place that we were thrown from. Part of the battle is in accepting the fact that we can't go back, that because of the losses we have incurred we are in a new place that gives us the option to stand and fight the uninvited change, or journey forward. There is no going back. Sometimes the sun doesn't rise.

Sometimes the Sun Doesn't Rise

"In this world you will have trouble. But take heart! I have overcome the world" (John 16:33 NIV). Sometimes the sun doesn't rise. When it doesn't, we think that something is odd or wrong. Sometimes, the sun simply doesn't rise. That's the nature and manner of life. We fight because it's not normal when we need to recognize that what is not normal is entirely normal. Our idea of normal is typically the constructs that we have created that rule out pain and loss. We seek to build and insure the perfect life, thinking that somehow this will shelter us sufficiently against the realities that everyone else has to deal with.

Sometimes the sun doesn't rise. Sometimes it doesn't rise for days or weeks or sometimes much longer than that. Life just does that. Our attitude should embrace both the loss of our sunrises and an anticipation of the fact that the sun will rise again. It may rise differently or in some manner not quite the same as those we have known before, but it will rise.

Hope is bred in the darkness, for in the light hope is unnecessary, or at least not as necessary. Sunrises that don't happen create the very place for the breeding and nurturing of hope. Anne Lamott shared a similar sentiment when she wrote, "Hope begins in the dark, the stubborn hope that if you just show up and try to do the right thing, the dawn will come. You wait and watch and work: You don't give up." Sunrises that don't happen give us a chance to work these very things out in the recesses of our souls. Darkness forges character and tempers the steeled strands of our souls. The sun will eventually come up. However, in the meantime let the darkness do its work.

We all travel in the darkness at times. Sometimes the bulk of our journeys are in darkness. At those times we most often choose not to travel at all, but to postpone or forestall the journey until it's light again. When the sun doesn't rise in our lives, our posture is to stop and wait until it does. The stopping is usually engulfed in fear, a sense of injustice, anger, a fatalistic attitude, or some other such negative and destructive emotion. But what is missed is that fact that we shouldn't have stopped at all. We should keep on going, darkness or not. Darkness should not halt the journey. We go forward anyway. "To travel hopefully is a better thing than to arrive," wrote Robert Louis Stevenson. The traveling is the most important thing; therefore it should not be halted.

We need to assume a wildly bold posture of believing that when the sun does rise, it will rise with a brilliance and intensity we have not known previously. We should take the radical yet entirely realistic risk of believing that pain and loss throw open the windows of the soul and wipe clean the smudge from the heart, letting us see what we could have never seen or conceived before. We forget the fact that loss geometrically enhances our appreciation for life if we seize it instead of letting it seize us. It stirs us deeply, shocking us into the realization that what we have taken for granted was not something owed us, but a gift granted us. Loss obliterates a toxic sense of entitlement, reminding us that we are privileged travelers in this life, not people living on that which was owed us.

Sometimes the sun doesn't rise, and in many ways we should be terribly grateful for that. We should be grateful because getting our way does little more than keep us safe and comfortable. Out of safety and comfort emerges mediocrity. And out of mediocrity emerges a life never stretched, rarely celebrated, and heavy with everything moribund and lifeless. Sometimes the sun doesn't rise, and maybe we should be thankful for that.

A Sunrise Anticipated

When the sun doesn't rise, our focus is solely on the fact that it didn't and it doesn't and it won't. It becomes all about what is not rather than what might be. Life moves one thing out to move other things in. However, we assume a posture based entirely on loss, where something was stolen and we stand forever unfairly pillaged. We myopically stare at the gaping hole left in our lives and see nothing but the hole, not realizing that a hole is defined by everything around it that is not a hole. Typically that which defines the hole is much larger than the hole itself. Rarely does a hole define or describe the larger part of anything, except when we define it as such.

We are not open to terribly restorative options, to the life-altering reality that God is "making everything new" (Revelation 21:5 NIV). Implied here is that things get old. There is a deterioration and subsequent change that is natural. In time, everything will be old, and yet out of that which is old, God designs something new. Therein lies the principle. Things will become old. We will incur loss. The sun will not come up at times and we will walk around with cavernous holes. It will happen. Yet, that which is old creates space for the creation and implementation of that which is new.

Old always ends and begins with new, not the other way around. Old is temporary and momentary and we should embrace it as such. Storm windows are put up, worlds close down, sunrises stop, and we find life both confining and dark. Rather than see these times as omens for something new that is certain to arrive, we focus on a world shut down and a sunrise that didn't happen.

Whatever is new is tried and tested in the fires and flames of that which was old. God is about the business of creating, of moving in a manner that is ever-enhancing and creative. It's much more than simply replacement, of swapping out something to replace something else that was lost. In our losses God has space to take that part of our lives to the next level, to interject and birth generous and marvelous enhancements that we would have never imagined nor even remotely conceived. Sure, sometimes the sun doesn't rise. But when it doesn't, in time it will rise again in a manner superior to any other sunrise that we had been privileged to before.

As Benjamin Disraeli put it, "Grief is the agony of an instant, the indulgence of grief the blunder of a life." The grief of it all in the span of our lives is only an instant in duration. "Weeping may stay for the night, but rejoicing comes in the morning" (Psalm 30:5 NIV). To indulge in something that is passing is foolishness. Centering ourselves on what is coming, that eventual sunrise, is to temper our losses with the greater gains yet to unfold. It's realizing that the storm windows will come down, the world will open itself from horizon to horizon, and the sun will rise on those very horizons.

It is here that we can grieve the sunrises lost, yet hold in balance an anticipation of sunrises yet to come. It is realizing that "you can't have a light without a dark to stick it in" (Arlo Guthrie); that without darkness we would not appreciate nor understand the wonder of light. It's an odd blending of loss and anticipation, of learning and appreciating, where we have hope enough to grieve and grieve enough to hope.

Light Enough

I really don't know when the sun rose again. All I know is that it wasn't for a long time. Emotional darkness is infinitely darker than any night that nature can paint across a nighttime landscape. If it's dark inside the heart, it's dead dark everywhere else. Sometimes the darkness seems more like a wall of black, impenetrable and pressing upon us on all sides. Sometimes the dark seems so dark that it pulls the very oxygen out of the air, it pins us in a place where we can't move, and it has such a leaden weight to it that it presses us flat and immovable. Sometimes it sucks the very life right out of us, leaving us limp, anemic, and entirely incapacitated. Sometimes the darkness is much more than simply dark.

Darkness is powerful, which makes it feel supreme. When real darkness descends, it is so encompassing and debilitating that we can't imagine anything that could counter it. It is so devastating that rescue seems impossible. If we get out of it, it's because it simply passed like a thunderstorm or it was finished with us or it found something else that gained its attention. But controlling it or finding some means of getting out of it feels entirely impossible.

But God is in the darkness. The darkness may remain dark, but its power is stolen. It's dark, but it's robbed of everything that made it dark. In the darkness there was enough of God to navigate the darkness of Mom's passing in a manner that seemingly incapacitated the darkness. It was an odd dichotomy where darkness prevailed yet it was navigated as if it didn't exist. It was not a realization that I had at the moment. However, looking back I realize that I navigated the darkness better than I sometimes navigate in the light. That is the stuff of God in the darkness.

"Even the darkness will not be dark to you; the night will shine like the day, for darkness is as light to you" (Psalm 139:12 NIV). When God joins us in the darkness, the only person in the darkness is us. All is as undiluted, absolutely perfect light to God. We can know that there is a sure compass, a steady hand, an undiminished eye, and a vigilant guide that walks with us.

In the terrible oddity of it all, I found that leaning on God as my guide rendered my own vision completely unnecessary. I floundered because I couldn't see and then I realized that when partnering with God, not seeing is perfect vision. In fact, God's vision in my darkness is infinitely better than my own vision in the best of light. It is my sense that I saw more in the darkness than I saw when it was finally light. And in the strangeness of a relationship with God, I never missed all the cold and suffocating things that darkness is, but I do miss not being forced to rely on His vision, as it is infinitely superior to my own.

Is leaning on God something that is temporal, that we work to remove ourselves from in order to reassert our independence? Is God that spare tire or crutch whose stint in our lives is only designed to hand life back to us once we are ready to resume control?

Or does leaning on God expand who and what we are as we borrow and draw sustenance from His perfection in order to deal with the consequences of our own imperfection? Is there not incredible joy, boundary-less living, markedly expanded vision, and insatiable hope that leaning on God imports into our lives? I found it to be exactly so.

Even though the sun eventually came up and the storm windows came off, I somehow grieve not having that terrific and wonderful reliance that allowed me to grab God, and to have Him grab me. In the wonderment of God seizing me, the vistas of my life were thrown open. I prefer not to be on my own, not because I crave dependence or am weak. It's not that I like the darkness, because I don't. Quite the opposite. I crave the unity with God where He breathes Himself into me and I am exponentially expanded beyond my senses, my capacity to feel, beyond any idea of what life could be like. Darkness put me there and in that I am terribly grateful for the darkness.

Sunrises that don't happen leave darkness. God is present in the darkness. It seems that He is emboldened by it, seeing it as the perfect place to display the fullness of Himself in lives that can see no fullness because of the inky blackness that they are submerged in. "Even in darkness light dawns for the upright . . . ." (Psalm 112:4 NIV). The light dawns because God is in the darkness. And when the light dawns, we are awed that it is so many things we never previously knew it to be until we had journeyed without it.

This precious light in the thickest darkness and the discovery of it is indispensable in helping us make the surreal real. It is through God's eyes and His light that the surreal nature of our losses is exposed sufficiently to make them stunningly real and inexplicably meaningful.

CHAPTER 8

Making the Surreal Real: Embracing the Contradictions

While grief is fresh, every attempt to divert only irritates. You must wait till it be digested, and then amusement will dissipate the remains of it.
  —Samuel Johnson

THE SNOW FELL EARLY. IT came uninvited and intrusive. Fall had not had its time or its chance. It had barely begun its fiery ritual when winter stepped in early, prematurely stole the stage with four inches of snow, and then retreated for a later time. It seemed a tease of sorts, yet it seemed entirely unfair.

The leaves had just begun to turn, still leaving the canopies full of summer's fading foliage. Caught unawares, limbs snapped under the weight of the wet snow as it drew down on a million surprised leaves. Nature seemed confused and disoriented, two seasons occupying the same space at the same time, not being certain what to do with each other.

As a kid, it was the stuff of magic as the seasons seemed to overlap, giving us fall and winter all at once. It was a double portion, the year pulling two entirely separate and distinct times together in one glorious collision. I couldn't figure out what to do with it as each season had its own traditions and ways of doing things and ways of thinking and ways of being. It was a grand contradiction where time seemed less one linear line and much more two lines running in parallel right over the top of each other at the same time in the same place.

Adults seem to lose the wonder of life, narrowing it down into something that must make some sort of sense. Life must run in predictable channels that are cut deep by life and experience. Whether life rages or simply flows in thin rivulets, it must always follow those channels. That fall, life ran way outside any of those channels. For an adult, it was an intrusion. For a kid, it was the stuff of magic and the relentless creativity that life spins around us, never quite letting us believe that we know it all.

I remember feeling in some sort of wonderland between two worlds, being part of both but separate from both. And here there was both a sense of wonder and yet a sense of the temporal, knowing that magic lasts only a moment but wonderment can last a lifetime. Life rushes out of those channels only briefly, so it was up to us to immerse ourselves in a moment that would soon draw down and away, returning to predictable channels that had no magic to them.

It wasn't about making sense of two seasons being present at the same time. It wasn't about the contradiction of it all and figuring out how to make sense of it. It seemed entirely natural. Nature extended us an invitation that we didn't have to figure out; we were simply offered the opportunity to enjoy it. And so we bounded into the basement and retrieved boots, thick gloves, and downy coats that seemed prematurely awakened and still drowsy. Donning our winter apparel, we charged out into the magic of two seasons being present at once, knowing that it would be gone all too soon. It was not a contradiction for a kid. Rather it was an adventure, something entirely new and a moment begging play and exploration.

Contradictions suggest that some thing or some event contains two facets that are irreconcilable. Somehow, there are things that cannot occupy the same space at the same time, making the moment entirely surreal. Certain things are mutually exclusive and therefore we have to separate them from one another rather than walk in wonder. We can attempt to sort it out, or we can embrace it as a new and unique opportunity to visit a rarely trodden part of life.

Sometimes in the vastness of life, God brings things together that otherwise could not be together. Sometimes God brings irreconcilable opposites together and for a moment lets us live awed in the possibility of the impossible. Lewis Carroll, in his book *Alice in Wonderland*, wrote, "Sometimes I've believed as many as six impossible things before breakfast." How grand and how freeing that is. As a kid, that's what I did.

However, too often our response is to live in confusion and horror, being panicked into somehow trying to make sense of what we should simply enjoy: fall and winter all at once. Robert Fritz put it well when he said, "If you limit your choices only to what seems possible or reasonable, you disconnect yourself from what you truly want, and all that is left is a compromise." What we think we want is to eliminate pain. What I think we truly want is to have this window that has been briefly thrust open to be something that stands contrary to our pain, that says that we have here, at this moment of terrible grief, the opportunity to expand the fabric of our spirit and our existence outward and upward in ways unimaginable. We want pain and loss to be worth something that is greater than the pain and loss. That is what I think we truly want. Anything else in the face of the horrendous pain and loss is pathetic compromise.

It's here, in these places, that we get a double dose of life and a glimpse of life unleashed from the confining fetters of our own constricted minds. In these times and places, God exponentially opens life for a grander glimpse than we could have imagined, if we would only pause rather than panic. That fall, I chose to pause.

An Adult in Contradiction

It all seemed misty, as some sort of dozing dream that we know to be a dream. The reality of Mom having been alive was still just that, a reality too rooted in my history to yet see anything other. All I knew was Mom alive. I had no other experience base to draw from. Mom now having passed was also a reality, but far too fresh and too contradictory to be embraced as reality. There seemed to be two parallel realities that merged simultaneously and ran over the top of each other in some sort of emotional void that wasn't big enough to accommodate both of them. Acceptance was barred by contradiction.

Losses create contradictions. The contradictions rest in the difference between what things were like prior to the loss, and what things are now like following the loss. At the outset of a loss, these two contradictory realities remain realities in our minds. The fact that they exist together when they should not or supposedly could not makes these times surreal.

Surreal in Contradiction

Sometimes certain places hold time, frozen and in bold relief. There are those places that time constantly adds to but where the thievery of time is somehow circumvented. Over time these places become a repository of history where a sense is developed that the history held by this place will only insure a future that is more of the same. Sometimes history is so thick in these places that anything other than the furtherance of the history held there is inconceivable. The house that I grew up in was one of those remarkable and sacred places.

Mom and Dad still lived in the very house that we had grown up in. There's something terribly emotional and inordinately vast about that. Walls ooze memories and moments, chronicling lives in both crisis and celebration. Every corner was packed precious with events that sat silently, patiently waiting to be recalled.

It seemed an old, patient farmhouse seasoned gentle and wise by nearly a century of time. A richly landscaped acre spread out about it as the hem of a long, resplendent gown that was woven rich with memories too many to be recalled. Over time, those memories had run together into some sort of intimate tapestry that invited recollection of the individual threads, but that had been woven with such intricacy that it was altogether overwhelming. It seemed sacred ground that was trod upon and cared for with the utmost respect.

In the center of it all there sat a snug living room, a maple and marble fireplace at one end and an ascending staircase at the other. It was framed on one side by a sunroom of expansive glass, and on the other a formal dining room set with furniture of crafted oak and trimmed in tasteful antiques. In the living room we had gathered on innumerable occasions. Christmases past had spun the living room a holiday delight of lights, trees, and packages wrapped in nothing but love. Here in this place had walked the likes of aunts, uncles, cousins, grandparents, and others who each added their own distinct uniqueness to our lives. In the living room I had watched an uncountable number of episodes of Captain Kangaroo, the landing of Apollo 11 on the moon, and the assassination of John F. Kennedy. History had played itself out on the old Zenith black and white television, the now absent console bringing history right into that very room.

Here, Easter baskets had been hidden. In that room we had talked about what my yet unborn brother's name should be. We cried and we laughed. We had celebrated and grieved. Nights came and days went with an increasingly fast-forward momentum that sliced through years as if they were but days made of thin mist. And through it all, we went as a family. Hand in hand, sometimes at odds and other times in a remarkable unity. It all happened right in the living room and the walls seemed to ooze testimony to every bit of it.

The night of Mom's death another memory would be added to the decade-stacked litany of memories. Sitting in a sullen circle rendered in grayish emotional tones, we discussed how we would take care of her that final time as she had taken care of us for so many years. The discussion was of funeral homes, burial costs, obituaries, and an ever lengthening list of family members to be called and informed of her passing. Who would lead the service and whether there should be a brunch to follow. It was indeed a surreal contradiction where time seemed less one linear line and much more two lines running in parallel right over the top of each other at the same time in the same place . . . much like that fall when winter ran parallel.

She was never coming back to the room in which we sat; the room was that largely of her love and making. Yet here we spoke of her passing. Her sacrifices and her commitment had largely made the living room what it was. Yet, she would never step foot in it again. The contradiction was insurmountable. It screamed with an emotional voice that made navigating the discussion and the decisions nearly impossible. It was unfathomable that we were doing what we were doing. Any shred of sleep was fitful that night.

Two Different Places in the Same Place

When we sustain a loss, we are thrust in a place between two realities: one of what was and the other of what now is. When two such perceptions occupy the same place, we are spun into confusion. Fall and winter occupying the same space was an adventure for a kid and something disorienting for an adult. Life is not clean. It's not tidy and always arranged neatly. Convergences create opportunity. "See, I am doing a new thing! Now it springs up; do you not perceive it?" (Isaiah 43:19 NIV). Here, in the confusion of the convergence, we have an opportunity to see a new aspect of life. Something happens that is entirely unique and free of the demands of each part that crosses the path of the other.

Grief begins in embracing both. It's about recognizing that life is big enough to include both without contradiction. It was imperative that I immerse myself in all that the house and yard and living room meant and to absorb with renewed vitality all the memories that saturated it. It was likewise vital that I let Mom go, that we speak of and plan for her death. In the odd and incongruent convergence there lay immeasurable growth. Terribly painful, yes, but infused with growth nonetheless.

Grieving is often stalled and stymied as we attempt to remove the contradictions that we feel rather than embrace both as part of the process. There is this surreal feeling that places us in the mire of confusion and disorientation. We cannot get out of this surreal, disorienting state because we're attempting to sort out and separate the contradictions, believing that our first task is in the sorting.

In reality, our first task is embracing contradictions as a natural and very normal part of life's journey. We need to engage the contradictions, to allow our minds and souls to expand sufficiently to encompass both, to rise to the challenge of life as abruptly and often unfairly changed. It is the stuff of the human spirit where in the midst of our weakness we acknowledge and act on our strength.

Living Boxes in Boxes

Loss does not bend to our definitions of life. It is not tidy, it is most often not timely, and it can be terrifying. Loss wrenches us out of the worlds that we have constructed. It forces us into greater living, to an expansion that is frightful and terribly intimidating. Loss screams that the reality of life is not the reality that we have painted in thin coats of belief over veneers of fronts and facades. It forces us out into the very reality that we have built our constructs to hold at bay and completely supplant in some sort of naïve denial that very reality. Most of loss is often not about loss but about the reality that it forces us to face.

Contradictions break our boxes very profoundly and deliberately. Contradictions are incongruent, yet they nonetheless exist at the same time in the same place. Contradictions smash our paradigms, leaving us scrambling to reassemble those paradigms. Loss and the contradictions that loss brings do not allow us to reconstruct our boxes. Instead, they force us to face reality, refuse to build boxes, and engage life in a manner wholly free of both our boxes and our desire to build them in the first place. Contradictions are nothing more than our inability to embrace a fathomless God working out the impossible against and within the very fabric of our finiteness.

The pain of loss masks the promise of loss. The promise is simply the opportunity to revisit life and what we've made it, to ascertain the suffocating boxes that we've erected around ourselves, and to begin building a life free of walls, barriers, and limitations.

"Opportunity is missed by most people because it is dressed in overalls and looks like work," said Thomas Edison. It takes work to break our boxes. It takes work to live as God designed us to live. It takes work to step up and do that which the majority of people around us never do. But loss presents us with that exact opportunity, and it is most certainly work of the most difficult sort. But the rewards are grand beyond comprehension, skirting the very edges of our understanding.

It is the stuff of magic and the relentless creativity that life spins around us, never quite letting us believe that we know it all. It comes wrapped in incredible pain sometimes, so much so that we don't see the gift inherent in the pain. However, it is life expanding, accelerating outward, and inviting us to catch the hem of this thing and move forward. Loss often comes with a grand contradiction where things seem less one linear line and much more two lines running in parallel right over the top of each other at the same time in the same place. But it is a double dose of life, telling us that life is much less linear and much more a diverse collection of living, breathing experiences inviting us to both savor delicately and wildly ride whatever the wave might be.

What It Means for Us

The most profound facet of all of this is the change that it brings within us and about us. Change changes us. The very force that change brings to bear by virtue of the contradictions that it creates and the demand that it makes that we both rectify and correlate these contradictions as a grand expansion of life changes us. It can do no other.

Martha Beck wrote that "any transition serious enough to alter your definition of self will require not just small adjustments in your way of living and thinking but a full-on metamorphosis."

The greatest challenges are not about the challenges themselves. They're about the changes within us that the challenges force and birth. When we stand facing the seemingly insurmountable contradictions that loss forces on us, it's about how all of that will bring unfathomable growth and maturation to our lives. In the end, it's about the wild and grand metamorphosis that God is working through us and building in us.

Savoring Change as Always Changing

W. Somerset Maugham said that "nothing in the world is permanent, and we're foolish when we ask anything to last, but surely we're still more foolish not to take delight in it while we have it. If change is of the essence of existence one would have thought it only sensible to make it the premise of our philosophy."

Loss cannot be separated from change, as loss naturally and obviously brings change. But change will pass. The impossible contradictions of sitting in a family room that oozed innumerable memories largely spun and woven by a mother whose funeral we were now planning drove us into some surreal place from which escape seemed also impossible.

Yet that moment and those feelings are no more permanent than anything else is. We may not enjoy the moment, but we can learn to delight in the opportunity to embrace another facet of life that, although grievous, is yet another part of life. Likewise, we can delight in the growth that such times are certain to bring if we grant them enough access to our lives. While that might entail pain nearly intolerable, the effects and rewards of the growth that pain engenders reap eventual benefits far beyond the pain that wrought them. Numbness creates a place of preparation for just such growth.

CHAPTER 9

Working Through the Numbness: Loss Backlights Living

The true traveler is he who goes on foot, and even then, he sits down a lot of the time.
—Colette

THE LEAVES FELL, AND THEN it rained. That doesn't mean much unless you add that the temperature dropped and the water froze stiff and firm, something like a crystalline diamond drawn flat and laid perfect. The ice of fall froze time itself, seizing the very hands of time and holding them fast. Oddly, they somehow didn't seem irritated by the pause.

Sometimes as a kid I wondered if time was really all that worried about keeping time, or was time more interested about what happened in its passing? Did God design time to keep everything in order by setting some cadence to life, or did He design it as a framework within which wondrous things were given a place to happen? Whatever the case, that fall the ice waylaid the turning of the seasons and fossilized it for a few days. It seemed that time stopped and created a space for magic.

Freshly turned leaves were sealed in layers of clear, crystal ice. There were none of the bubbles that typically give ice a whitish and somewhat porous look. It had frozen it the stuff of the finest crystal, clean and clear and utterly transparent. In its various panes, it had caught and sealed the electric leaves of fall, preserving them as amber perfectly preserves insects for thousands of years. Fall was put on hold. It seemed somewhat stunned and taken aback by it all.

Although caught unawares, fall had somehow decided to let itself be suspended. The seasons turn on time, exhibiting child-like obedience to a massively forceful yet entirely invisible clock. Somehow that same clock is set deep within each of us, giving us a clear sense of time and passing that leaves us knowing that the moment is precious because in a moment it will be gone forever.

Yet, despite the precision of seasons turning, nature made room for pauses and alterations. Nature was big enough and precise enough to know that imprecision and alterations were not a threat at all but an inherent good that elevated the need to pause and celebrate over the need to keep perfect time. In life, it's more about the pause than the precision. A life truly lived is not about keeping perfect time. Rather, life is about living perfectly in time. As a kid, that came quite naturally.

Sometimes you have to stop the advance of everything because what you're missing in the advance is not worth maintaining the precision that brought you to that special moment. Rush often results in waste and moments forever lost. Attention to time is inattention to the life that fills that time. So much can be lost. Yet that fall, nature stepped in and stopped the hands of its own clock . . . briefly. It seemed to step back, fold its arms in some sort of bemusement, and whisper, "Look at that!" And I did.

Baron Friedrich von Hugel postulated that "no great artist, no great philosopher or scientist, no great ethical striver will ever fully, consciously, and deliberately admit that what he strives to paint, to sculpt, to compose, or to discover or to understand, or to live and to be, is just human so-and-so-ness, very possible without any further significance or truth about it whatsoever." Nature screams that there is more, and it will stop itself to prove it. I often wondered if, to prove that very point, nature froze fall that year to force a closer inspection upon which we would be without argument that, indeed, there was more . . . infinitely more.

The cold, the very thing that stopped fall, was numbing indeed, drawing the cold center stage. I sometimes wondered if we paid more attention to the things that stopped time instead of focusing on what the pause was trying to show us. Adults saw the cold and the early ice as an intrusion, as winter being presumptuously early and wholly uninvited. As a kid, it wasn't about time stopping. It was about what time stopping did. It gave us some additional time to do some additional exploration and see what life would do with this pause and the gap that it created.

As a child, life always seemed to intersect my world in a way that superseded whatever reality I had grown comfortable with. It seemed to always give me a renewed and entirely fresh sense that any reality that I perceived was always superseded by a deeper reality. As a kid, there was always a sense that there was always more.

Life running relentlessly on a perpetual clock affords only enough time to see whatever lies in the moment because it confines us to that moment and that moment alone. The moment is but a wafer-thin piece of life. Most of life lies somewhere else rather than in the moment. It's when life stops and is held fast, even if it's for a mere breath, that we are freed from the confining tyranny of the moment to see just how much more there really is. Kids see these times and naturally leap into them. As a kid, I did. Especially that icy fall.

The cold and ice backlit the splendor of fall and held it for a few more precious days in crystal windows that preserved the miraculous in puddles and pools. That seemed to be the contradiction. Something so frigid and seemingly insensitive held fall fast long enough to savor it a bit more. And as a kid, savor I did until the weather warmed, the ice melted, and the hands of time were freed.

The Cost of Holding

"In all things of nature there is something of the marvelous" (Aristotle). These times seemed to recognize the magnificence of that truth, deeming it necessary to hold the splendor of autumn for a moment longer. It seemed, however, that what held time was also cold and biting. It numbed autumn. I suppose that was the price of stopping time. Holding something in order to savor it does not come without cost. We view being numbed as uncomfortable. We see it as uninvited and bothersome. Yet it held the flame and fire of fall for a couple days more, making the numbing tolerable, even invited.

And so as kids we spent hours peering into puddles turned to caches of time held fast. The world seemed to stop just for us, to give us an extended glance at wonder before it would dissipate, rolling back into and catching up with the turn of seasons always on the move. It seemed that we had been granted some extraordinary privilege where nature halted for a bunch of kids; that in the frigid numbness something precious was given a few more days to be savored by children enamored with something they couldn't understand. And it was done in the numbness of an unexpected winter.

Numbness Misused

"If you don't risk anything you risk even more" (Erica Jong). Working through the numbness means moving toward feeling. Many of us live in an intentional, suspended, and elongated numbness where not feeling is preferred to feeling. We wouldn't necessarily quantify it as numbness, nor would we admit any tendency to perpetuate it. But living in the denial of our permissive numbness likewise allows us to live in denial of our pain. We can then assume normalcy at the expense of normalcy. That's numbness misused.

"Go in the strength you have" (Judges 6:14 NIV), says God. Risk feeling your pain; risk sorting through your numbness even though that action frees your pain to be felt. Numbness that remains numb has no means to be resolved. Not risking means that you risk even more. Risk in whatever strength that you have. But as part of that process, recognize the unsuspected place of numbness in grief and loss.

The Correct Use of Numbness as an Adult

Do we recognize the pause in the numbness? Numbness is a forced pause, temporal and eventually passing in time, but it remains a pause. Is it possible that there is purpose, even profound purpose, in the pause? And so do we fight numbness because it numbs us, or do we hide in numbness because it's a better state than one of pain? And in doing either of these, do we miss the treasure of the pause that's inherent in numbness?

Sometimes the numbness is the space that gives us the time to prepare to embrace our losses. It's not the place to hide, but the place to prepare. It seems to be the pause that allows us to catch our breath, steady ourselves, and prepare to move into life with whatever loss we've incurred. It's a place where we have permission to not focus on our grief, but to refresh and equip ourselves to eventually engage it. It gives us a necessary place to prepare when we otherwise might not.

Numbness gives us a forced permission to gather our resources both internally and externally before engaging and embracing our losses. It's the staging ground wherein we suit up before heading out to feel the force of our loss and wrestle our pain into obedient and productive submission. Numbness is a precious stop on an often precarious journey.

The entire backdrop had changed. Most of Mom's death had been framed by the hospice, the gentle pond brimming thick with waterfowl, and the deep painted woods that held the hospice close.

Now everything moved to the mortuary. Here the finality of her passing could not be denied nor hope any longer be held out. A hospice holds out some hope, despite how irrational, that death might not come. It fans a tiny cache of thinly burning embers that it might all be a mistake, that a miracle might happen, that the doctors may have been wrong, and that death might not be ready just yet. A hospice doesn't foster those emotions. It simply creates a pause sufficient enough for the indomitable hope of the human spirit to dare to hope.

A mortuary holds out no hope as it confirms death beyond the reach of the most rigorous denial. Clearly, in a mortuary the embers are cool and ashen gray. The entire culture, language, business, and even mythology of a mortuary is built on the frank reality of death. The societal process of concluding a death is then formalized to sterility, extracting much of the emotion inherent within it. It permits numbness and begets it all at once.

A mortuary both manages and displays the terminal nature of life. John Donne wrote, "Any man's death diminishes me, because I am involved in mankind." The corporate diminishment of a single death is felt in a mortuary. It seemed geometric in that the death of Mom somehow became infinitely multiplied by the death of so many others as a result of the binding sense of corporate humanity that flooded that place. That magnified diminishment, coupled with the evidence that a mortuary exhibits that life is terminal . . . it was all numbing.

The mortuary was itself embraced by deep woods and the blaze of fall much like the hospice. In the oddity of life, it stood directly across the street from the church at which the funeral would be held. Somehow, it marked this autumn transition from the wake of waiting for death in a hospice, to formalizing it in a mortuary, to finalizing it in a waiting church.

The day had warmed, rubbing the colors a bit misty and aromatic. The sky had been scrubbed a pristine blue, clean and nearly crystalline in every direction. Held as a sparkling backdrop against the brilliant colors of fall, there was something entirely clean and wholly untainted about the day. Even in this place, geese drew across the ocean-blue sky, sometimes in handfuls of cloistered travelers, at other times in massive assemblages of airborne aviaries.

It seemed that fall was settling into itself and doing quite naturally what it had done for eons. In that, it appeared to have accepted and embraced Mom's death as something entirely natural, now moving on with unabated ease. Sometimes you know that grieving a loss is being done right and admirably, but it's so natural and easy that it seems to be disrespectful or naive of just how big the loss has been. Fall almost seemed to be doing that.

The mortuary itself was clean and formalized. A buoyant yet respectful receptionist. A knowledgeable, gentle, and precisely thorough consultant. A tightly mapped plan of procedures that moved in a logical and reasonable progression, distancing everything we were doing from a death to a wisely and reverently constructed plan.

In the mortuary were all the things that confirmed death, each step and every tedious decision driving home the reality yet too fresh to embrace. It was a place of blurring incongruences where each step expanded the chasm between the familiarity of life and the complete unfamiliarity of death. The wider the gap, the greater the numbness. Yet the numbness made way for the procedure and allowed the emotions to gather themselves for the time that the formalities would be concluded and the loss embraced.

Fighting the Numbness

Numbness seemed to be something to be fought. Standing knee-deep in the sludge of death's impaling losses, the decisions now being ruthlessly demanded as a result of those losses and the looming transitions now unavoidable, in it all numbness seemed to be wholly escapist and unashamedly disrespectful. It generated the wrenching dichotomy of providing an escape that was both desperately needed and yet felt as desperately selfish all at once.

It was now about a modest maple casket with a soft and intimately embracing cloth interior. Tiny ceramic angels, ornate, tender, yet gently commanding, fitted on the four outward corners of the rich-grained maple. How to dress Mom. What jewelry to put on her. Making decisions based on presenting Mom in a manner that was truly representative of who she was. Doing little things that symbolically represented pieces and parts of her life. Including variant nuances that celebrated bits of history that were cherished. Embalming and details appropriate, yet gruesome. Headstones, inscriptions, burial plots, and state regulations demanding adherence to various ordinances spelled out in cryptic legalese.

We had not had time to consider how to summarize her life. The death itself was entirely consuming, leaving no room to conceptualize how to draw seventy-nine years together and display those years in three hours of ceremony and burial. It dramatically accentuated loss, ramming the scope of it all to the forefront in such a hurried fashion that it could not be conceptualized, embraced, or digested.

Sometimes life rams us. The force is such that to embrace the entirety of it all at once is impossible and possibly lethal. Such forces are capable of overwhelming the sum total of all the accumulated and amassed resources that we have to counter and manage those forces. Sometimes it's just too much.

Numbness can provide a vitally needed refuge that permits exposure to aspects of the forces that are assailing us, while refusing to grant others entrance. It can mercifully reduce our cognizance of the events that surge around us. In the space that numbness creates, we are granted the ability to navigate what we must at the moment and prepare for what we must face in the future. Numbness can be a reprieve, a sanctuary wherein we prepare.

God in the Space

In the oddity of it all, I found the numbness of a mortuary and all the assorted trappings of death as well as the loss that filled its rooms as a place where God showed up entirely untouched by the numbness itself. Numbness had the power to isolate me from everything that was not God, and in doing so it appeared to create a place especially for Him.

It seems that numbness is God's way of clearing the heart and mind, sweeping aside all that would impede His having a uniquely powerful encounter with us in a uniquely devastating time. It makes for an empty room cleared of everything except two chairs and time. Numbness is God's invitation to intimacy in crisis. It's a secluded hovel in the deep dark. It's a moment in time, a place where life can be frozen much like the leaves that fall. It can all be stopped for a moment to savor, to take one final look at the glories of what has passed in order that it might be celebrated before we move on to winter.

While numbness was temporal, as it should have been, it provided a needed refuge to gather my strength, clear my head, shake my heart free of the darkness, and grieve. Without the numbness, such preparation would have been impossible. Without the preparation, the events to come would have been stripped of the immense growth that they held.

The numbness held time frozen long enough to celebrate and pause, to find a place to gasp and then breathe in the gap where the hands of time were briefly and graciously halted. It was nothing of escape but everything of reprieve and preparation. Without this place of numbness, the role of the pheasants that was to come would have never been achieved. I would have never recognized what was to gather along the fence line of my life. I would have entirely missed what God was yet to gather around me and the golden blessings that would be liberally poured as a torrent of love and recollection into my loss.

CHAPTER 10

Pheasants Along the Fence: God in the Stubble

I no doubt deserved my enemies, but I don't believe I deserved my friends.
—Walt Whitman

AS A KID, FALL SEEMED like a transition much more than a season. It had a brevity about it, that whatever happened during this season was much more a movement from one place to another than actually being a place itself. That made it all the more special. Things happened in the fall that didn't last long, that came and went so you had to enjoy them while you had them. The pheasants along the fence were one of those magical, temporary things.

In the fall, massive combines of leviathan proportions would comb the endless farm fields around our house, harvesting the bounty of spring's plantings and summer's work. Fields of corn stretched all the way to hazy horizons where the masses of both earth and sky met in a thin, indistinct line. The corn rendered the land an ocean of green stalks that rippled in long waves when the wind blew across them. In many places the fields drew up to the edge of stalwart tree lines as if the sea of corn formed an estuary and challenged the oaks, ashes, and maples in some sort of silent standoff. In the fall the stalks transformed to a dusty gold while the trees burst into color, each bringing an added brilliance to the other.

The combines seemed as the leviathans of the fields. They gorged themselves on the endless sea of corn and moved through the shallow estuaries that ran alongside the woods. There seemed a savagery about them, a complete lack of respect for anything other than their appetites. They would run for days, disgorging their stolen bounty in large trucks that gorged themselves full, driving off to unknown destinations only to return famished and selfish yet again. So it seemed to the kid that I was.

When the combines ran, they would flush out an assortment of secretive wildlife that had made the fields and the sea of corn their home. It seemed that a panic ensued in the fields, that an unnatural anomaly stepped into the natural and sent the sea of corn into a tsunami of turmoil. Animals fled pell-mell to whatever refuge would embrace them and shelter them.

What the harvesting leviathans flushed out more than anything else were the pheasants. Graceful, royal, and demure, they would burst into the air ahead of the land-borne leviathans in coveys of power and brilliant color. Somehow there always seemed to be more of them than anything else. They lent something of spice to the fields, meaning that they had to be sufficiently scattered about to lend something of flavor to the sea of corn.

As a kid, I felt that the sea of corn gloried in them, shed tears that lapped the shoreline of the fields when they left, and begged them back when the leviathans had left for other waters. The fields were never the same without them, so they always returned. But in the meantime . . . .

There's always something in life that I was enamored with. Sometimes it made sense, and other times it made no sense at all.

Life is often like an attic packed tight with the stuff of both treasures and junk. Yet in some abandoned corner drawn tight with
cobwebs or hidden behind a mountain of brittle and crumpled
boxes there's something that may be entirely worthless but entirely captivating.

As a kid, among other things it was a large quartz rock, an In-
dian head penny, and a collection of rubber bands. Small treasures
whose value lay not in anything monetary, but the pleasure that
they gave a small boy. Their value was not set by money, but by
meaning . . . two facets that are in most cases entirely contradictory. Pheasants were much the same.

I was always enamored with them because of the creative genius
so deftly manifest in the ornateness of their beauty. Somehow it
seemed that God had kind of cut loose when He designed pheasants, His pallet having spilt on them with God deciding not to
clean up after Himself. There was a sort of majesty and royalty
about pheasants, in terms of both their color and their sleek form.

When flushed, they would burst into the air in a blur of elegant
feathers and brilliant color, beauty revealed in rare glimpses so as
not to be tarnished or taken for granted. It was a combination of
their beauty and mystery that haunted me and irresistibly drew
me to them, like a piece of something divine that you'd give anything to touch while knowing that you can't.

They lent something desperately needed to the fields; like the
trim on a coat can bring brilliance to the rest of the coat, so did
pheasants bring a silken trim to the fields and our fence.

During the week the combines combed the adjacent fields, harvesting the sea and adjacent estuaries that lapped the woods' edge.
The pheasants would flee the metal teeth and deep-throated die-
sels, finding refuge and a temporary bit of solace along our back
fence. The span of the acre that made up our yard put them far

enough away from our house to give them sufficient refuge. The densely wooded yard next to us gave them cover when needed. In return, they gave back mystery, a sense of glorious aloofness, and an unparalleled beauty. It seemed that the divine visited us, or so it felt as a kid.

It was in the mornings mostly. They would walk the back fence, strutting back and forth along its length as if biding their time until the combines had worked the fields and retired from the sea of corn until next fall. For a kid, the magic and the wild of the fields came right into our yard, into our world. You knew that there were some thickly mystical things out there beyond the boundaries of the fence that surrounded our yard. The world was a big place loaded with mysteries equally large and mostly bigger. But we didn't really anticipate that mystery would come into our yard and our lives.

You learn to see magic and wonder as the stuff that's out there somewhere in some distant place. You think you have to imagine it from a distance like in books or movies or songs, touching it through the experience of others. Mystery seems elusive and distant, too mysterious to be right where you are. But when it showed up right in our yard, it was almost unfathomable.

We had two ceramic likenesses of pheasants on our fireplace mantel. But they were just images of something from another world that had to be mimicked in ceramic because the real thing would never show up in our lives. We try to fashion mystery and magic in whatever form or relief we can, our thirst for something more driving us to create shadowy images of it because it will never come close enough for us to actually see it. But they did.

Relentlessly, fall after glorious fall, the pheasants would show up at harvest time. The season was turning, the corn was cut, the sea of fields was laid bare, and the magic of the pheasants would appear strutting the back fence line. In a time of turning, when life was shutting down and gathering itself in for a pending winter, the glory, wonder, and mystery of the pheasants would show up. I would grab the old binoculars and pull the pheasants up close as they paced the back fence, capturing magic in two lenses. Things were dying and magic showed up. As a kid, it was both magic and magical.

An Adult and Friends

Sometimes in life things happen where the fields and hedgerows of our lives are ravaged. It doesn't seem much like some sort of harvest or a new season in our lives. Rather, it seems utterly destructive, the mindless devastation of the seas and estuaries of our souls. Some leviathan of some sort shows up and we are utterly helpless before it. We're taken right down to the ground and then whatever roots remain are dug up and ground down. It all seems more like death than harvest, ravaging rather than reaping.

A funeral is a strange thing in that the planning and the actual carrying out of the service keep the service focused on the formality and format rather than on the loss that gives it all purpose. The numbness of your own emotions and the formality of it all leave you going through a series of orchestrated motions for sixty foggy minutes. It seems terribly painful but inordinately surreal all at once.

The season had turned. Mom lay in an ornate maple casket lined with soft, white fabric edged in lace. Candles flickered; voices spoke in hushed tones of sorrow and empathy, lending some slight fill to the massive void that engulfed the chapel. Everything seemed to move slowly as if reverence demanded that all is cautious and soft.

The leviathan had shown up and long since left, leaving in its wake stubble and soils lacerated. Mom was dead. The fields of both my heart and soul were bare, being nothing more than the stubble of memories and emotion. There was no magic.

We had expected a small group of mourners that morning. Somehow we had settled in our minds that this would be the case. We had no reason to believe or suspect otherwise. Most of her friends had been long dead themselves. Other friends had long since moved and set out on other courses that sent them to other places and unknown horizons.

Yet, as the time for the service approached, they came anyway. Friends aged by time and friends who had been lost to time. Acquaintances of various sorts from various places. Others whose lives Mom had somehow touched or impacted. Some of them were people we had entirely forgotten about, having surrendered them to another time, those divergent journeys, and other places. But they came, flushed out of the fields of life and settling along the fence line of our hearts for a few moments.

They came with dream-like magic and wondrous mystery, all of which was unexpected. The funeral became flooded with the recollection of sweet memories long forgotten, rich times experienced jointly in a manner that binds hearts and souls regardless of time and distance. Innumerable journeys shared that bind people regardless of how far away those journeys take both them and you. Whatever the sea that had been ravaged, conversation after conversation inundated it with fresh, warm, and familiar waters.

It was a raucous gyration, being thrust from times and people in recent memory, to those of the distant past, to some in between. It was connecting aged faces with what we remembered them looking like before the years had drawn them by time. Reconnecting people and times and events that had fragmented and become entirely disconnected over time, catching up with lives lived out outside ours. It was the wild ride of emotions, from warm memories to deep affection to laughter to tears and then back again. The fencerow of our lives was filled with people, memories, and warmth too numerous for the fence to give space to it all. I was joyously overwhelmed.

It was life resurrected: the entire lineage and history that God had graciously granted coming back in assorted pieces and parts all at once through the love, conversation, and recollection of a hundred friends and family members who had been flushed out of the fields of our lives and who walked the back fence of our hearts and our circumstances. It was more than magic. It was life lived in a concentrated form, all the wonder and pain and love and moments distilled into a hundred conversations that blew through my life at that funeral.

It was friends and family. It was about the community of people around me, many who had become invisible or distant. All of them had a part of me in them, a memory or a recollection or a thought, shards of something precious. And they brought themselves and those pieces together at one time in one place at one moment along the fencerow of my life.

The combined force of it all offset my loss. It reminded me of the life granted to me, the people who made up that life, the power of their love and weight of their presence. It reminded me that a field rendered nothing more than emotional stubble was rich in ways I could not have imagined.

The service was to begin. They were all ushered into the chapel, leaving warm and sweeping wakes in my life. It seemed that the sum total of my existence had coalesced in a handful of moments. All that was sweet and wonderful and rich, treasures long lost and forsaken to time were drawn from the wells of these people and poured lavishly into my life to the degree that I almost couldn't stand. The oddity of it all was that in the midst of a solemn funeral

I was filled to abundance in a way that I almost couldn't tolerate for the sheer joy of it.

With the guests seated, we had one more opportunity to bid Mom farewell before the casket would be closed for all time and rolled into the chapel. The tidal surge of love and memories that had swelled around me was in actuality her doing. She had woven many of the friendships. She had encouraged so many of the events and relationships that I had just relived in those glorious moments outside the chapel. She had shaped and honed and protected that world which so many people recited to me. And because these people were flushed out of their lives and had chosen to walk the fence line of my life for that hour, I was given more than that which Mom's death had stolen.

Fields Flushed

The fields of our lives will be flushed. When it happens, the magic and the mystery will find the fence lines in our lives and walk there. We don't look to the fence lines because all we see are devastated fields. To our utter detriment, the fence lines where things gather are ignored.

Our focus becomes enmeshed in the swirling questions of *why* and the issue of justice or injustice. The sense of being the victim, of the cruelty of life descending without conscience or remorse occupies our minds. We commit to restoring the fields, or we retreat in seeing such a mission as entirely impossible, or we set about to expend all of our resources in the construction of some new field somewhere else.

But we neither give notice nor heed to the fence lines. What has God allowed to be flushed out of the fields? What precious things, things of mystery and magic, has He brought out of the devastation and loss that are handed to us, things that are brought right into our lives if we scan the fence lines rather than grieve the fields?

In the divine logic that seems so humanly illogical, we are freely handed mystery and magic. Yet it seems too simplistic and insufficiently grand, so it's tragically bypassed. The things flushed from the devastated fields that we all have are often precious things we have lost or forsaken or carelessly discarded in our journey. The foolishness of errant decisions or self-centered actions incurs costs for all of us that leave wreckage, remorse, and loss in their wake. Yet these things can be redeemed in the blessing of the fence lines that are, in times of crisis, flushed full of all that we threw away.

The things flushed to our fence lines are things that we are given the priceless opportunity to redeem if we so choose. Opportunity always emerges from loss. Loss is never an entity entirely unto itself. It is always interwoven with opportunity. We simply don't see those threads because we assume them not to be there. Therefore, we don't look.

Devastated fields are often littered with the losses that have diminished our lives and robbed us of any opportunity to redeem those losses. Sometimes those losses are death. While the devastation in our lives is certainly devastating, and sometimes devastation of the greatest sort, it flushes our lives and hands us second chances . . . terribly precious second chances. And those are flushed to the fence line of our lives.

Part of our loss, then, is seeing the gains and then seizing the gains. We are given the privilege of restoration, of precious parts and people once lost now restored. Of decisions and choices and actions once grieved now regained.

"I will repay you for the years the locusts have eaten—the great locust and the young locust, the other locusts and the locust swarm" (Joel 2:25 NIV). In the devastation of the fields, whatever

the locust may be for each of us, there is the promise of restoration. Watch the fence line. See what is flushed out and gath-
ers there. Embrace the opportunities and seize the mystery of a
relentless God who is an utterly relentless opportunist on your
behalf. And it is His relentless nature that allows us to position
ourselves to celebrate our losses. It allows for the great bonfires,
the unleashing power of prayer, and wild culminations of lives
lived and handed to God.

CHAPTER 11

A Bonfire and Prayers:
The Place of Prayers and Praying

Do not pray for easy lives. Pray to be stronger men. Do not pray for tasks equal to your powers. Pray for powers equal to your tasks. Then the doing of your work shall be no miracle, but you shall be the miracle.
  —Phillips Brooks

BY THE TIME FALL HAD spent itself in a consuming blaze of fiery fury and raucous celebration, it seemed to find itself tired in a way that made tired good and warm and welcomed. Nature had shed itself of all the glories of a season now passed and honorably observed.

It was time for a well-deserved winter's sleep that would draw together energies sufficient to repeat the glory all over again next fall. Seasons know no end. They only know the raucous and simultaneously subdued celebration of whatever glory is theirs, compounding that glory in knowing that the glory will be revisited with just as much vigor on the turn of the calendar. Nature celebrates "what is" in the certain confidence of what will come.

The crowning mantle of leaves that had given the trees body and bulk now left sleepy skeletal remains that rolled off to stilled horizons. The emerald greens of an energetic summer had burned red, orange, and yellow in fall. The trees had now lost their electric colors. Mottled brown leaf litter lay thick in the deep woods and liberally spread across the expanse of our yard. As a kid, we had to rake it up.

Most things that entail work seem to go on forever when you're a kid. Play lasts but a moment, the joy of it all seemingly gobbled up by time. Work lasts an eternity as if time has no taste for it. Raking up an acre of leaves was work; it was the clean-up following a most joyous party that nature invited us to each fall.

Fundamentally, the system to the clean-up involved three things: a huge navy blue tarp, an old, tired Sears lawnmower, and massive metal rakes that kept getting gummed up with handfuls of dried leaves. Performing such a massive job was really less about simple tools and more about willing hearts. The magnitude of what looms before us in life is much more about the state of our hearts and much less about the size of the challenge. Such was the job of raking up an acre of leaves.

With the large, hungry rakes and the electric vitality of childhood, we would fill the old tarp as full as conceivably possible. The tarp itself was obediently tied behind the aged lawnmower with a few frayed cords of worn-out clothesline. It all seemed a partnership of sorts: people, a sputtering piston engine, and hand tools united in the solemn purpose of bringing fall to the close that it was worthy of.

As we walked alongside the tarp, the old mower would pop and rumble its way to the backyard, spewing blue-gray smoke and dragging the leftover confetti of fall's celebration to a garden now vacant. Here the contents of a season exhausted and spent in the celebration were deposited. The cycle of mower, tarp, and leaves would go on for an entire day until we had assembled a massive pile, remnants of what had been.

As a kid, it was the final act of this season. Fall could not clean up after itself. That part was left to us. Somehow it all seemed right and appropriate, that if we were privileged to have had a part in it all, we should likewise be something more than free-loaders simply enjoying it all and then walking away. It was recognizing that this part of it all was really a terribly small price to pay for what autumn had invited us to and lavished on us. In some sense cleaning it up seemed more of a thank you—the paying of a reverent and deserved homage to a friend now gone.

Everything seems big when you're a kid. The gargantuan pile of leaves was no exception. It was almost ceremonial as we would invite a neighborhood full of our friends over, find long sticks upon whose end we would affix multiple marshmallows, assemble several buckets of water just in case, and gather a box of wooden matches. We would patiently let the day go dark, often with the stars littering the ceiling of the galaxy above us, themselves waiting with electric anticipation for the grand bonfire.

Then Dad would begin the process of lighting the mammoth pile. It was something of a holiday, a sacred moment, and a rite of passage all in one, those moments when something is so indefinably good that it is simply indefinable and therein something of the divine.

The head of a spindly match would be briskly drawn across the sandpaper side of the matchbox, spewing a few scant blue sparks in its wake. They would be followed by a blue-white flare that would quickly settle into a single flame. Cupped in Dad's thick hands, the flame would gain strength before Dad touched it to the pile.

With the nurtured flame illuminating cradled hands, Dad would quickly move around the massive pile, softly lighting it at various places around its base so that it would burn evenly. I always marveled that what took months to produce, that had provided shade to playful children and refuge to a ceaseless army of birds, that had sung with the wind and joyously turned its face to summer rain, burned so quickly. These leaves had flared the world with colored finery that splashed to every horizon roundabout and beyond. Yet they burned in almost an instant. How could something so precious be consumed so quickly?

Flames, ever the opportunists, sent wavering fingers of yellow and orange up the sides of the pile in some sort of consuming climb. Underneath the pile, they seemed to run their fingers in order to gain enough of a hold to heave the pile upward. It was as if the flames themselves cupped the colossal mountain of leaves in flaming, ever strengthening fingers and lent their force to lift the pile to heaven itself.

At the thundering peak of it all, a prolific dance of spirited sparks spun upward from the flames as if attempting to find their place among the brotherhood of the stars that appeared as sparks themselves. Spinning and whirling, they ascended in shifting columns of ashen smoke, rising above the treetops and out of the reach of my imagination. It seemed that God opened a giant door in the underside of heaven itself and drew the sweet incense of fall into heaven's halls and marbled corridors. Somehow it all felt mystical and right and good.

The pile of leaves was engulfed in flames in but a few seconds, roaring with abandon and with what seemed like great glee. The fire didn't seem concerned with pacing itself and savoring the fruits of fall's remnants. Somehow it seemed that the celebration was something like a prayer that was too glorious to contain and too expansive to hope to moderate. Prayer is sweet abandon to God that is itself entirely without parameters. The flames seemed to illustrate that with force and great glory.

With this surge of marvelous energy having quickly dissipated within several minutes, the flames drew down from a shout to a mere muted whisper, eventually settling into a mass of glowing embers that cooled quickly in the chilled fall air. It was suddenly dark and silent. The prayer of the fire seemed to close in an expanse of silence that was the perfect "amen" to all the wonder that had just transpired.

We ate the marshmallows that we had been able to roast in the brevity of the flame, raked the embers into a collected pile, and then doused them sufficiently with water until they could be heard no more. With fall now finalized, we headed to the house and waited for winter.

Prayer of Fire as an Adult

"The smoke of the incense, together with the prayers of God's people, went up before God from the angel's hand" (Revelation 8:4 NIV). Such are the prayers at the close of time. Prayer at the culmination of something grand seems massively powerful and uncompromisingly appropriate. It's the intentional importation of the divine from which everything in existence finds its origin on one end of life and its sole destination on the other. At the end, prayer both acknowledges and delivers everything to its rightful place. It takes the remnants of the life celebrated, instantly wraps God's fingers around all that the person was, and thrusts them heavenward and homeward.

Mom was all about prayer. Her life had been infused by it and she had saturated our lives with it. She made it real by living it, which is the only way that makes saying it real. Abraham Lincoln wrote, "I remember my mother's prayers and they have always followed me. They have clung to me all my life."

Even though Mom was gone, her prayers were not. They outlived her, seeming to actually become more powerful in her absence, filling the space she left in excess of the space itself. Prayers are timeless and entirely without boundaries to inhibit them. They carry a bit of those who prayed them with them, seemingly stamped with some indelible spirit of those who uttered them. They live beyond the point that we do. Prayers are speaking something eternal into the finiteness of our existence as a whisper that will not succumb to the seasons. I could hear the whisper of my mom.

Prayer is nothing of the passive recitation of various petitions that dissipate like smoke in a breeze. Such things are human babble, not the forever fabric of prayer. There's something uncompromisingly eternal and lasting in the words of a prayer, something that clings long after the prayer has been spoken, and something that remains infinitely beyond the point that it is forgotten. Prayer is the ageless stuff that we set in and against everything that ages us. It's what lasts when nothing else but God does. Prayer grounds the finite in the infinite so that we're not hopelessly bound to a hopelessly short existence on this dying planet. Mom's prayers did that. I could hear them still.

Now Mom's body lay dressed, perfectly groomed, and extravagantly resplendent in a rich maple coffin engulfed in generous white linens and edged in delicate lace. She seemed perfect, that somehow this perfection had always lain under the simplicity that was Mom, much like magnificence lies under the simplest prayer. Flowers surrounded the coffin in bountiful colors of spring, a season yet to come, a season that prayer fully sees and aggressively prays into existence.

All the remnants of her life had been gathered over the past few days: insurance paperwork, an accumulated history for a sullen obituary, wills reviewed and assets dispersed accordingly, memories pooled and shared from various persons both near and far. Brittle photos in tattered black and white relief and edged in aging browns captured wondrous bits of her, raking those pieces all together in a marvelous collage. It had all been raked together in some sort of reverent pile much like the leaves of childhood. All had been gathered.

After greeting numerous friends and other mourners, we walked into the sanctuary, took our seats to the sound of a thoughtful piano, and waited. A funeral is about waiting for something that you don't want to wait for because you don't want it happening in the first place. I sat in the front row, pressed my elbows against shaking knees, and prayed the kind of prayer that is more about reaching for something to hold on to rather than praying with some kind of identifiable intentionality.

The funeral itself followed by the graveside ceremony was all less than three hours. A life of seventy-nine years was brought to finality in a burst of minutes. It was all perfect, holding Mom in the esteem that truly represented who she was. It was embraced with tears and the emotion of shared humanity when certain events bind us together in ways that simply don't permit division. It was all marvelous: blurred with churning emotion but marvelous nonetheless.

The finality of the graveside was stunning and yet nearly impossible to grasp. All of the seasons of her life as reflected in the accumulated mass of memories and moments shared seemed collected in a rich maple coffin that lay under a pure white canopy over a freshly dug hole yet vacant. It was all raked together here, all seventy-nine years gathered in this single place.

One person's life is simply too vast and has too many miles and too many memories and far too many moments to be completely assembled at one time in one single place. If it could be done, I would completely doubt the ability of any one place to fully contain the mass of it all. Such a task would seem so impossible, so imposing, and so exposing that it would be wholly disrespectful.

If somehow a single life could be entirely gathered in a single place, it would seem to suggest that that life had not been lived, or that a road had not been walked, or that a journey had been entirely forfeited. How could something as expansive as a life suggest otherwise? And yet, how could a life be otherwise celebrated? For it would be entirely unfair and somehow derogatory not to celebrate every bit of it.

Standing at the graveside with my father seated in front of me and with my hands on his shoulders, I wondered how this moment could not embrace all of Mom. Less than six feet in front of my father stood the casket holding the remains of the woman that we all desperately loved and who had loved us with a deep mix of desperation and inexplicable passion. It seemed that Mom and these many bystanders of both this moment as well as the many moments of her life would be cheated if the entirety of her richness were not somehow brought together in great glory at this moment. We could do that with the leaves of fall, and it was glorious. But doing it here seemed frustratingly impossible.

Some things are divine in such a way that they can fully embrace unembraceable contradictions, irrespective of the enormity and mass of their differences. Call it magic or call it majesty. Call it what you will, but it happens in divine moments.

At that moment, standing in the middle of that graveside ceremony, I wanted that to happen. I couldn't have articulated that at the time because words fail terribly in the grandest moments of our lives. I have found that grandeur is irrefutably diminished if we attempt to imprison it in the confines of language. Grandeur and the stuff of godly majesty must be left free to soar through our souls at spiritual altitudes so lofty that words simply cannot survive. At those heights, the oxygen of human logic and reason has long been depleted and we must surrender to a language of the soul for which words do not exist.

The Victorian poet Coventry Patmore wrote, "The more extravagant and audacious your demands the more pleasing to God will be your prayer; for His joy is in giving; but He cannot give that for which you have not acquired a capacity; and desire is capacity." If desire is the capacity, then my desire to have Mom fully celebrated provided a capacity large enough for the entirety of a marvelous life to find room.

And here the pastor prayed. It was unlike all the others, as the others seemed oddly preparatory. This prayer seemed final but incredibly expansive and engulfing. His words escape me except that room for the entire expanse of Mom's life was somehow opened up in a manner beyond his words. I was caught in something of awe.

A prolific dance of spirited sparks seemed to spin upward as if attempting to find their place among the brotherhood of the stars. Spinning and whirling, they ascended in shifting columns of a simple pastor's prayer, rising above the treetops and out of the reach of the imaginations of all gathered there. It seemed that God opened a giant door in the underside of heaven itself and drew the sweet incense of Mom into heaven's halls and marbled corridors. Somehow it all felt mystical and right and good.

It seemed that all of the gathered memories and mementos of Mom's life were engulfed in flames in but a few seconds, roaring with abandon and with what seemed like great glee. With this surge of marvelous energy having quickly dissipated within several minutes, the flames drew down from a shout to a mere muted whisper, eventually settling into a mass of glowing embers that cooled quickly in the chilled fall air. It was suddenly dark and silent, the pastor's prayer concluded under a gentle white canopy ruffled by a gentle autumn's breeze surrounded by fall's flame.

We savored the memories of Mom that we had been able to enjoy in the brevity of the flame, raked the embers of those memories into a collected pile, and then doused them sufficiently with the water of a hundred tears until they could be heard no more. With fall and Mom now finalized on this side of eternity, we headed to the house and waited for winter.

Prayer in Our Loss

Paul says, "Pray without ceasing" (I Thessalonians 5:17 ASV). The less than obvious implication is that there is never a place where prayer does not belong or would be insufficient. Life can never be too big for prayer. Prayer will always be able to cast a net wide enough to embrace and thereby engulf anything spun and woven by this world. Prayer stands as the undefeatable resource that is always larger than whatever it is prayed into, or prayed over, or brought against. It is an irrefutable tool of God that champions God's purpose and champions our lives.

Prayer embraces and engulfs our losses. It allows us to celebrate them in their entirety, while releasing them in their entirety. Like the leaf piles of fall, prayer brings culmination, celebration, and reverence together at one comprehensive moment.

The loss then takes on a different perspective as a prayer genuinely spoken makes all look different. It sets the stage to leave the loss and then venture forward. Prayer prepares us for walks in life's deep woods and opens us up sufficiently to embrace a vibrant and victorious future that God passionately desires to escort us to, and a future where He is likewise fully present and eagerly awaiting us.

CHAPTER 12

A Walk in the Woods:
Walking into the Future

For man, autumn is a time of harvest, of gathering together. For nature,
it is a time of sowing, of scattering abroad.
—Edwin Teale

AT SOME MAGICAL, INDESCRIBABLE, AND largely unpre-
dictable point, fall reaches it zenith. Rose G. Kingsley wrote, "In
the garden, Autumn is, indeed the crowning glory of the year,
bringing us the fruition of months of thought and care and toil."
Sometimes in life things peak; expected or unexpected they peak.
"The fruition of months of thought and care and toil" mystically
yet quite intentionally comes together and swells to a wild cre-
scendo. As a kid you don't recognize the peaks. All you know is
that something terribly special is transpiring and you've somehow
found yourself in the middle of it.

When you're a kid you don't question what you're in or why.
Life is still so fresh and new and breathtakingly unknown that it's
about taking it all in, like breathing fresh morning air that's so
perfectly fresh that you don't have room or space to do anything
but breathe it. As a kid, you haven't developed a lot of compari-
sons yet, so it's not about something being compared to some-

thing else. There's an inherent freedom just to enjoy something for what it is and not how it stacks up to whatever it's being held up against.

As a kid, these kinds of peaks were all too overwhelming in a wondrous kind of way. The power of life having unleashed itself all around me left no room to ask why or how long it all might last or what I should do with it other than immerse myself in it. It seems that true celebration is missed when we analyze the celebration itself. Kids don't do that. They simply take it for what it is and enjoy it.

And so those days came when life peaked, when everything around was something like a full moon magnified a thousand times and then some. It seemed some sort of good and right pattern where life was supposed to peak, and when it did I had to grab it, hold it with all my might, and press it deep within me until it passed from my grasp. When it did pass, I was left with the wild exuberance of having lived a special moment, coupled with the sadness of its temporal loss.

The loss was never the focus, as the expectation of the next culmination was simply too overwhelming and whimsical and exciting. It was then about waiting with wild anticipation until the next time it all peaked so that I could grab it and do it all over again. Life was not about losses. It was about celebrating culminations with the innocence of abandon and then peering forward with squinted eyes and intentional hearts in order to attempt to make out the next one.

Something about the change of the seasons, nature on glorious fire, persistent geese etching a mystical but powerful background to it, and winter waiting on a frosty horizon for its eons-old cue to enter the flow of the seasons—as a child all of that left me spell-bound and mesmerized. Sometimes life coursing within the very veins of your soul renders you so wildly and helplessly alive that you think you're going to die because the sheer wonder of it all is going to kill you. When life really peaks and the wonder of it all distills in one place, it becomes something of the divine and therefore something infinitely beyond our capacity to embrace. In these places and at these times we are helplessly in love and hopelessly alive. That's living.

I had no room or need to question anything or ponder any of the stuff of life or seasons turning on the axis of a planet in transition. All I could do or wanted to do was soak it in until its goodness overpowered me and I had to let go or I'd explode. And so I held on until I couldn't. In the midst of having the wind knocked out of my imagination, I would catch my breath and wait for the next one.

In it all, life begged, or better it demanded, space away from it all. The reality is that most often it's not getting away from life but getting away from ourselves in life. As a kid there wasn't much of self there yet, so there wasn't much of a need to get away. In fact, the innocence of untainted hearts and eyes allowed me to embrace life and myself despite the crescendos, both good and bad, that fell around me.

As adults, we seek out those places and times of innocence that give us permission to stay wherever we are. As a kid I never had to flee because innocence afforded me a place to embrace both life and myself. It may be some sort of naïveté, but I would prefer to see it as innocence granting us a place and space to engage life more honestly since the biases of adulthood have not tainted us sour when we don't need to be.

An Adult and a Walk in the Deep Woods

Mom's death finally had some sort of closure. We had embraced the first few shards of stinging acceptance, that our lives were now void of her presence, her love, and her innumerable graces. The funeral was visually clear but an emotional blur, rendering it a memory oddly powerful for all of its fuzziness and indistinct tones. The graveside service had mystically summed it up, tying her life up like a glorious ribbon on a grand package.

For the first time since her passing there was some thin piece of desperately needed closure. For the first time there was some sort of desperately needed inkling that life just might go on, albeit in some yet unknown and possibly unwanted form.

Mom's death had not come to a complete culmination just yet, rendering it a loss and nothing more. It threw us squarely into some blackened, primordial limbo from which escape or eventual departure seemed to discount the loss altogether. It was entirely too fresh and fiendishly raw to even remotely entertain the idea of life without Mom. We assumed ourselves eternal captives to our loss.

But for this moment, for the very first time since her graveside farewell, there was now a place to rest for a bit and catch a breath that had so long eluded us that it seemed we had forgotten how to breathe. Satchel Paige once said, "Sometimes I sits and thinks, and sometimes I just sits." We were ready for sitting minus the thinking.

In his poem "Autumn in the West," William Davis Gallagher wrote,

> *Out in the woods of autumn! I have cast*
> *Aside the shackles of the town, that vex*
> *The fetterless soul, and come to hide myself,*
> *. . . In thy venerable shades.*

Dad needed to get away, to get away and sit in the venerable shades. The funeral had been the day before, a mere flicker of time yet a gaping chasm of emotion not yet twenty-four hours removed. Something about a forced finality held captive in a maple coffin and the peaking of a season drew Dad and me away to the woods, that place where the shackles could be cast aside and the fetterless soul find a place to hide itself.

The Necessary Escape from Ourselves

Sometimes we need to escape from the human experience, as there are times when there is absolutely no relief if we remain in it. The breadth of our personal and corporate resources is far too drab and altogether too shallow to provide any sufficient buoyancy or sustenance during the difficult times. Our own biases and the tainting of adulthood mean we can't go there on our own. We must go elsewhere. So we went to the place where God's handiwork is prolific and His presence profound. We went to the deep woods.

There is something sacred about walking among the wooden behemoths, especially when they are deep and thick. Ash and oak, maple and cottonwoods—muscular giants that seemed to hold the sky aloft so that we could tread safely underneath. Randomly interspersed meadows ran waist-high in waving fall grasses, giving a royal blue sky ample space to stretch out and take stock of itself. Tepid creeks thick with crystal waters softly meandered around sleepy rocks, gurgling over velvet green mosses and deftly skirting under the vegetation that embroidered both banks.

Saint Bernard of Clairvaux wrote, "You will find something more in woods than in books. Trees and stones will teach you that which you can never learn from masters." The woods were masterfully masterful, steeped in the sacred in a way that escapes words either grand or miniscule. It's the kind of deep sacred that can be ascertained only in the fathomless recesses of a heart completely quiet but entirely raucous and noisily alive at the same time.

The forest was fully ablaze that day, utterly on fire in a way that readily diminishes the most brilliant fire. This kind of blaze was not consuming. Rather, it was totally beneficent, selflessly giving in every aspect, holding out to the willing observer the opportunity to share in what life looks like when all the accumulated energy and vitality of life itself culminates in a single spectacular instant. It was the grand culmination of a forest vibrantly spawned in spring, grown resplendent through a generous summer and bringing it all to a glorious culmination.

It was something like an eon of sunrises occurring all at one indescribable moment, blinding, each capturing every conceivable aspect of every sunrise that has ever fired an eastern sky. Something of the brilliance of the sun, the crystalline air, a lucent blue sky, and the soft warmth of the day seemed like a divine celebration that was incredibly loud but whispered all at the same phenomenal moment. It was a glorious culmination where all were invited to observe and to share.

"The true beloveds of this world are in their lover's eyes lilacs opening, ship lights, school bells, a landscape, remembered conversations, friends, a child's Sunday, lost voices, one's favorite suit, autumn and all seasons, memory, yes, it being the earth and water of existence, memory," wrote Truman Capote. Dad was inundated with the kinds of memories that prompted celebration rather than regret. There was a pleasantness about it that allowed the loss to be released and the assemblage of warm memories to coalesce into a culmination much like that which fall was exuding and cheering all around us.

In getting to a place that allowed us to get away from ourselves, to free ourselves from the chains and shackles of our own tainted humanity, the process of culmination was allowed to take place. We could not have done it without a walk in God's deep woods.

Culmination as the Finalization of Loss

Walking in the woods with Dad, dead center in fall's glorious transition, it became increasingly clear that we are prone to see loss only, not culmination. We see the loss clearly, but we completely miss the outcome of loss which gives sustained purpose and desperately needed meaning to the loss.

It seems that the order to things in life involves loss. Loss is concluded and completed by culmination. Culmination celebrates and brings to fruition all of that which was lost. Culmination allows something to be completely finalized so that whatever is new has uninhibited access to the entire landscape of our lives and our futures. As God will say at the end of time when this life reaches culmination, "I am making everything new" (Revelation 21:5 NIV). "New" follows loss, leaving loss ever hopeful and never vacant.

Loss was really a reversal, a celebration of what was coming. It peaked in a sort of culmination that made its celebration and departure complete. Loss was not to be centered on the loss nor was it designed to be so. Loss was and is the preparation, the clearing aside, the making room for something grander that was on its way. "Autumn is the mellower season, and what we lose in flowers we more than gain in fruits" (Samuel Butler). Any loss is outweighed by the gains, even though our pain typically blinds us entirely to those gains and their stout magnificence.

In no way did that diminish the grief and horrific pain associated with loss. It simply gave it meaning in the present and meaningful purpose for the future. Culmination says that loss does not stand alone nor is it relegated to the scathing injustice of meaninglessness. Loss meant something . . . yet unseen because of the way that pain clouds the present and totally obliterates the future when it hits us. But a grander purpose is more certain than the pain itself. Culmination allowed the loss to move aside for a future unclear yet entirely certain.

Moving Aside for What?

It was all too clear in nature. The woods would soon move fall aside for winter. Winter would eventually do the same for spring. However, what makes loss hard for us is that we don't know what it's moving everything aside for. We don't have the information or the insight or the vision or the energy to shift our gaze forward to the sweeping horizons ahead of us and attempt to discern what's now coming our way because of the room that loss has made. Therefore we can't build up some sort of anticipation because we don't know what to anticipate. We don't know what this is all making way for. As the writer of Proverbs so aptly said, "Where there is no vision, the people perish" (Proverbs 29:18 KJV). And in loss we feel like we're perishing because we don't have the vision to see past the loss.

Robertson Davies made the astute observation that "the world is full of people whose notion of a satisfactory future is, in fact, a return to the idealized past." Our vision is more about what we think we had, rather than what in reality we can have. We tend to live in a past full of unresolved losses that tie us and leave us bound there, when an unfettered future lies ahead. In all of that there is no sense of any direction because there's no hope that there is one.

Too often we hold to a past that we've renovated or entirely reconstructed. We frequently take great liberty with our pasts, cutting, pasting, sanding away the rough edges, and sprucing it up a bit. At times we are so rigorous that we come to believe that the past we have fashioned from the raw realities of our past is the real thing when it is nothing more than a piecemeal fabrication. What we then hold is not so much reality, but what we have molded from whatever reality really was. We hold something less than fully genuine when a future stands before us that can be completely genuine.

"'For I know the plans I have for you,' declares the Lord"— plans that are entirely embedded in the reality and brazen boldness of a God who is uncompromising and zealous in His love for us, a God who is unrelenting in His commitment to working out the wildness of godly adventure in our lives—plans that are intended "'to prosper you and not to harm you, plans to give you hope and a future'" (Jeremiah 29:11 NIV). It's not about holding on to an idealized past embedded in unresolved losses. Rather, it's about believing in the reality of a future that's as grand, divinely turbulent, and notoriously wild as we will allow God to make it.

Something of that inherent sense and call came over me during that walk in the woods with Dad. Beneath canopies of stellar oaks, ashes, and maples the thoughts came in unrelenting torrents. Nature is God's throne room, the pinnacle of His terribly creative genius. God is present everywhere at all times. But in the woods He is present amongst His creation, rendering Him and the manifestation of His Being in one place simultaneously. Nature oozes God. And in those places I can do no other than look forward because God is the Creator, always creating, always advancing, always moving forward and making what is to be much more than anything that was.

It's when I embrace that reality that loss becomes the fodder of the future. That doesn't diminish loss or make that which was lost any less important or valuable. It does none of that. Rather, it infinitely enhances the value of that which is lost because it is the very thing, the quintessential material, the essence from which the wonder of the future can be constructed. Loss is terribly painful, but it is gloriously rich and forward looking. Fall was preparing for winter here in the woods, a blazing celebration of what was to prepare for what will yet be.

Culmination as a Compass into the Future

In a speech delivered at Harvard University on September 6, 1943, Winston Churchill said, "The empires of the future are the empires of the mind." In a similar vein, Proverbs 23:7 states, "For as [a man] thinketh in his heart, so is he" (KJV). What we will do and who we will be will largely be determined by what we think. Will we be the idealized manifestation of our past if we choose to stay there, hemmed in and entirely imprisoned? Or will we be the ceaseless manifestation of everything that God designed us to be? Will we be bold enough to allow culmination to bring closure to our loss, or will we accept such a mental concoction as denial and embed ourselves in the past?

Loss puts us at this critical crossroads. Will we look backward to what the autumns of our lives are leaving behind, perpetually living stalled and stagnant in the rearview mirror of our existence? Or will we look forward to the horizonless horizons that these losses are making way for? Will we embrace and allow ourselves to be immersed in the culmination of that which was lost as a means of clearing the landscapes of our lives for the horizons of the future, or will we languish in the ever descending loss? Will we root ourselves in an idealized past, or will we cut ourselves loose and abandon ourselves to a God Who is uncompromising in working out His loving and living genius in our lives? The answers to these questions will prove nothing less than monumental.

A Grand Culmination to a Grand Future

It's an odd thing indeed. Kids are free of the encumbrances of knowledge and experience. We would surmise that their ability to embrace life with only a marginalized knowledge would likewise marginalize their experience. Ignorance is not necessarily bliss, but knowledge sterilized by pure rationale strips life of the miraculous and deadens its heartbeat.

Sometimes we need to stand aside and make way for the miraculous. Sometimes we need to give life the audacious permission to live outside the suffocating restraints of our understanding. Sometimes we need to exercise faith enough to believe in what we can't see and to invest in the very things that defy our imaginations. Sometimes we need to let things come to a culmination that relinquishes a cherished past and sets us on a course to an unknown but completely charted future.

That is the eventual purpose and terminus of grief and loss. It's the destination that pain desires to take us to. Grief, loss, and the accompanying pain are both the fuel and fabric of a grand journey if we let them be. Their ultimate destination is to "grow up into him in all things, which is the head, even Christ" (Ephesians 4:15 KJV).

The woods create a space to get away from ourselves. In doing so we subsequently lose ourselves in the deep and remote places of God where everything is in eternal culmination in order to make way for eternal creation. How can we achieve Christ-likeness in any other way?

Here, in these deep and reverent places, we see the future bolder, more brazen, and infinitely more brilliant than we could have imagined. Culmination paves the road for creation. And the journey on that road to that destination is measured and constructed by the very self-same loss that initiated that journey. In the oddity of God's design, loss paves the road to the created "next" that is always out there. It fashions that next step that, when taken, moves us one step closer to being like Jesus. It's walking where He walked.

And it is in these very places that we can fully celebrate what we had because of what "we had" now gives us in its stead. Life steps aside for life. In doing so we can celebrate both what has stepped aside and what now stands before us. And in this is great and unsurpassable celebration.

CHAPTER 13

Celebrating What You Had:
A Gift That Lives On

Death is more universal than life; everyone dies but not everyone lives.
—A. Sachs

EVERY FALL SCHOOL WOULD COME as surely as the leaves would turn and depart. The old, seasoned brick school buildings seemed to gently shake themselves awake after summer's lazy days and long, tepid nights. Having been free of the romping herds of children for an entire summer, it seemed that the buildings needed to reorient themselves a bit and be reminded of their roles. The initial migration of teachers and various staff roused the building from a summer's slumber to the call of fall and children hungry to learn or not.

With school racing toward us from the unrelenting pages of the calendar, Mom would round up her three boys and head off to the store to buy a few articles of school clothing, a pair of new shoes, paper, pencils, crayons, a ruler or two, graph paper, and whatever else would give her boys every edge she could give them academically. In the heart of a child it was a bemused mix of terrible sadness and heartedly denied anticipation.

Among the other things we got during this annual fall ritual was a shiny new lunchbox. Back then they were the metal kind with some sort of cartoon or superhero character emblazoning the front and wrapping themselves around all four sides. It was typically ablaze with color and action. Inside would be the old glass thermos, something that predated plastics, composite materials, and today's thermal foams. A flimsy metal latch of sorts somewhat tentatively held the fragile thermos in place.

The metal lunchbox was a repository of Mom's love, a small box within which she poured a bit of herself every day. There was always a sandwich, the inside layered with some sort of something from peanut butter and jelly to bologna to contents at times entirely unknown and suspect. It was typically framed on both the top and the bottom by the squishy, soft white Wonder Bread that we loved so much.

It was always about variety with Mom—a different sandwich each day unless we made a specific request. Chips. Some sort of fruit or vegetable and a cookie or something sweet to lend a flavorful touch to it all. On holidays there would be treats that reflected whatever the season was. They had a tendency to last far beyond the season, bringing the holiday back to us weeks after it had ended. Often there was a note, something simple but terribly meaningful like "I love you" or "Have a good day." Mom came to school with us every day in the form of love prepared and packed in a small metal lunchbox.

Yet, the most meaningful and at times emotionally wrenching part of lunch was the dime. That single shiny dime that would be scotch-taped to the inside of the lid. That single, daily dime was for the purchase of milk: white milk Monday through Thursday and chocolate milk every Friday . . . a single silver dime.

I cried over those dimes many times. They embodied great sacrifice—the real and raw kind of sacrifice that was not a one-time action of superficial charity. Those dimes were not the product of someone's fleeting sense of compassion or momentary intersection with their own humanity and that of others. Charity is too often driven by something less than something authentic. Too often charity and sacrifice are fueled by guilt, or a sense of what we're supposed to do, or the press of expectations that we're too ashamed not to fulfill. In such instances, it would be better to do nothing, as false charity is nothing other than humanity turned toxic.

But that was not the case with the dimes. Not at all. Someone decided to go without so that I could go with. For Mom and Dad, it was nothing of sacrifice, for real sacrifice doesn't feel like sacrifice at all. Rather, it feels joyous and wonderful. It was a resource possessed by loving parents who intentionally forfeited what was theirs so that I could have what I couldn't possibly get on my own. There is something terribly courageous, bold, and fearless in those kinds of attitudes, where love is not afraid to love. There is something divine when that attitude is turned to action. Such were the slim silver dimes that appeared daily in my lunchbox.

In the reality of our lives, a dime was a lot. It represented my Dad's hard work, my Mom's sacrifice, the giving to the children which meant Mom and Dad would go without. It was the stuff of selflessness that was performed day in and day out without ever viewing the act as selfless. It made me feel terribly safe as I knew that Mom and Dad would sacrifice whatever they had to in order to keep us safe. I was aware of the fact that life was frighteningly lean and precarious at times. But I knew that our needs would always be met because Mom and Dad would sacrifice at whatever level would be necessary to meet those needs.

An Adult and Cemeteries

It all settles into a surreal state in a cemetery. The hospice, the lingering death that finally came, the mourning family and hovering friends, the preparation, the funeral, the graveside service, a walk in God's woods, the discordant life set to an alien cadence . . . it settled here.

It was Christmas by the time I got back from an October burial. The road from October to December had been paved with thousands of miles of travel, hundreds of hours in session with hurting patients, endless hours of etching feelings and philosophies in the script of writing, moments of deep loneliness and suffocating grief. Now I was back. Snow covered the grave and spread a thick cloak of cold silence across a naked landscape. Life itself seemed withdrawn, creating a large and wide space so that one could privately and intimately ponder Mom's life withdrawn. The space for contemplation was vast and endless.

It was a magical place because it all had coalesced here: the raking of the leaves of Mom's life into a glorious fire of celebration. It made this ground sacred in a way that all other ground was ever inferior. Winter seemed to revere it. Spring seemed to be waiting to celebrate it. Summer would lavish it. But for now, winter gave space for reverence and celebration.

Nature had turned wholeheartedly to winter, finding itself asleep and lulled to forgetfulness about anything painful or otherwise. It was an intentional rest, realizing that one cannot deal with life constantly, that reprieve is terribly vital and wholly appropriate. Nature seemed to recognize that the stuff of living requires the stuff of resting. As terrible as things might be and as demanding as the ascent of life might present itself, we cannot face it constantly nor press our weight against it all the time.

Winter is both rest and preparation. It is a time of rest from the expended energy of spring, the explosive growth of summer, and the harvested bounty of fall. Winter is nature weary with success.

Winter is anticipation and the subsequent preparation of what will assuredly come.

Winter is preparation to simply do it all over again. To heed an ages-long pattern where little is transformed into stunning abundance in every nook and cranny where nature is given space, provision, and permission to assert itself. It rolls through the months unrestrained and unleashed with a vitality that cannot be dominated. And here in winter, it rests—intentionally, purposefully, and completely. Such is the stuff of grief. Such was the journey that led from my mother's birth to this grave on a quiet winter's day. And such was I.

"We are made to persist. That's how we find out who we are" (Tobias Wolff). So nature persists and so must we. Mom was gone, and her headstone irrefutably bore both the loss and its permanence. However, my life did not end with hers. Rather my life was enhanced, enamored with, and even enflamed by the memory of hers and the legacy that she imparted within me. It's in the trials that both life's gains and losses generate that I find out who I am. It's in the dimes generously taped on the lid of my life that I am bestowed with the resources to build and live life.

This tremendous loss that I pondered in that deathly silent cemetery at that deathly silent time of the year tore and pulled at a soul still tender. But I was more of what I was than ever. I understood myself more than I ever before had. It was odd that I hurt with a pain that words could not surround or define, yet I was more of who God created me to be than I had ever before been. And it was from the pouring of this woman's life into mine, both in dimes and in things far grander, that I was in large part who I was in that cemetery that bitter December day.

A Point of Reference

Life has many points of reference. There are those rare and special places that are like markers in time, standing perfectly still and entirely unmoved so that we can return to them and by point of comparison see how far we have moved, if we have moved at all. Nelson Mandela astutely observed that "there is nothing like returning to a place that remains unchanged to find the ways in which you yourself have altered."

Mom's grave seemed to have stopped in time, refusing to move forward. The culmination had been so complete and the closure so encompassing that time had stopped at this plot in the vastness of a cemetery now held in winter's embrace. I realized that I had not stopped, that I had trekked and ventured forward, in many ways unbeknownst to myself.

The stopping in time did not relegate Mom or her death to the ever fading annuals of the misty past. Rather, it gave me a permanent point of reference that would stand for the remainder of my life. Almost as if it were a gift, I now had this place from which to chart and measure my own progress.

Mom would not be lost. Rather, she would occupy the place in my life that she had prepared me for. Graciously and sacrificially, she had endowed me with the fullness of everything she was and had in order to equip me for life. Now, she became the very benchmark by which I measured the progress I would achieve utilizing the very gifts that she gave me. Much like dimes religiously taped in my lunchbox every day, Mom's gift to me would go on. Loss had a perpetual meaning. The dimes dropped into my life in torrents.

To Visit but Not Live

The temperature had plummeted the night before, leaving the snow layered with a crusty surface much more like ice than snow.

It seemed to lock winter in, to set the season as firm and unmovable, much like Mom as that benchmark.

But had I not allowed it all to culminate in this very place two months earlier, the benchmark would have been entirely irrelevant. Mom's life lavished me with innumerable resources to grow a grand life. Mom's death handed me grief and loss unparalleled that were in reality the gems and jewels that afforded me inestimable opportunity to grow. Her death then provided me a benchmark by which to measure the progress of it all.

And so, what appeared to end at her death was barely a beginning. An end is barely the beginning of a beginning. In God's economy loss is dramatically offset by the gain seeded in the loss. Mom gave me years' worth of dimes in the many lunchboxes that I carried over those many years and will carry in the many years ahead. Yet her life was not fully appreciated until she was gone, for only in the loss of her did the fullness of her have room to be what in the earthly confines of her body she could not be.

The Destination of It All

The destination is both simple and complex. The destination for all of us is to be shaped into everything God has designed us to be. It's ridding ourselves of terrible compromises and the cancer of mediocrity. It's about refusing to let the culture set the cadence of our lives and daring to believe that the impossible is simply the possible in disguise. It's about rising to a challenge that we can't achieve and embracing it anyway. It's about refusing to let ourselves reach our own funerals someday having been so much less than we were meant to be and could have been.

Grief, loss, and the pain that accompanies them can be devastating. Nowhere in this book has that been marginalized or discounted. What has been advocated, however, is that there is tremendous growth in tremendous pain. The whole journey as outlined in this book is a journey of excruciating pain and supernatural growth all in one. It is both indeed. The end of it all is Christlikeness. It's taking the worst that life can hand us and recognizing that it's often the most phenomenal stuff life can hand us. And it's in all that stuff embraced, as difficult as that is, that we grow in ways we cannot imagine.

Dimes in lunchboxes is what it is. Sacrifices turned to our gain. God Himself strewing innumerable dimes with gleeful abandon into the most grievous pain that we can imagine. Each dime holding within itself ample promise and endless opportunity. That's how God works. Whether it's colors turning early, front porches, storm windows, friends along fence lines, the bonfires of prayer, or innumerable other places, God is casting dimes everywhere. May you find the priceless dimes scattered everywhere you look, because in grief and loss they are always, always there. And they are there for you in your grief to bring God's purpose to uncompromised fruition in your pain. May God turn your loss to great glory, great gain, and even greater godliness.

Conclusion

Time does not change us. It just unfolds us.
—Max Frisch

TWO YEARS HAD ROLLED BY, or more appropriately rushed by. Life is a river of sorts, both gentle and tumultuous. Either way, it rushes by, leaving us wondering where it went and what we did with it.

The bronze headstone was now seasoned, having marked Mom's grave for two years. The grass had drawn up to its edges and wrapped the headstone in a sash of emerald green that lent an air of royalty to that place. The raised letters that silently spoke her name in bronze relief had weathered a bit, not in a way that seemed the stuff of aging, but rather the impartation of wisdom and serenity. The headstone seemed to have settled into its role of marking her final stop on her earthly journey and the stepping off place of an eternal journey in a perfect place.

Someone once said that faith is looking in the rear-view mirror. It's seeing how everything in the past makes sense when it's viewed from the future looking backwards. I didn't have that vantage point two years earlier when a group of mourners gathered under a white tent in this very same place. Traces of their presence had long vanished, each moving from this point forward in

different directions with their individual lives and unique journeys. Two years rendered the cemetery different. It rendered me
different as well.

There was something of grief accepted that found itself coupled
with a growth and maturity that was difficult to categorize. Times
change lives, and lives change times. Life moves on, the tenor set
by the times that we endure and the tone set by our reaction to
the tenor. The path away from this place two years earlier could
have set out in any number of directions. My response to an untimely death charted the course.

Yet it was the journey of death and loss, the embodiment of
pain exacerbated by all the assorted pieces and parts of such a
loss that forcefully drew me down with an inertia to thrust me
up. The journey did little to diminish my pain, but it did everything to grow me deep and tall while in the center of that pain.
I learned that the course of our society to eradicate pain at the
first hint of it highlights our inherent shallowness and forfeits the
monumental growth that the endurance of pain begets.

I chose to weather the storms and embrace the pain, a course
of action that I questioned more than once and more than once
regretted. I thought myself brave at certain times, entirely stu-
pid at others, and completely confused at times in between. Yet
somehow, someway, I stood. When I thought such standing to be
certain death, by God's grace alone, I stood.

And now I stood at Mom's grave two years removed . . . different, stronger, unexplainably richer. It was not that the journey
of grief and loss was over, for I'm not certain that it ever is. It's
simply that I stood and I was incalculably richer for having done
so. It may have been that aside from birthing me, Mom's death
and the gift of pain, grief, and loss spawned from that death was
the greatest gift she ever gave me. If that truly be the case, she

obviously didn't live to see it. However, I suppose that the greatest gifts of all are those whose riches the giver never sees.

The second to the last verse of the Bible reads, "He who testifies to these things says, 'Yes, I am coming soon.' Amen. Come, Lord Jesus" (Revelation 22:20 NIV). I suppose it's really all about that. Scanning a cemetery of thousands of headstones, I realized that this life is terribly temporal even though it pretends to be so much more. Because it's temporal, I must seize each precious opportunity to grow, to learn, and to allow God to take the heated knife of pain and use it to build me, shape me, temper me, and grow me into Christlikeness. Because, after all, if it ends in Christ, I desperately want to pursue Him in and through the entirety of my existence, as the pursuit of anything else is devastatingly futile and irrevocably a dead end.

"Come, Lord Jesus!" And in the interim, thank You for pain, grief, and loss. Not for what they are in and of themselves, but for the incalculable growth they induce and bring to my life and to the lives of those who are reading this.

May God bless your pain, your grief, and your loss in ways that manifest Christlikeness in you. May your journey embrace the riches that I have experienced in my journey as shared in the pages of this book. Indeed, may your journey far surpass my own.